Swift 3 Protocol-Oriented Programming

Second Edition

Build fast and powerful applications with the power of protocol-oriented programming

Jon Hoffman

BIRMINGHAM - MUMBAI

Swift 3 Protocol-Oriented Programming

Second Edition

First published: February 2016

Second edition: November 2016

Production reference: 1231116

Published by Packt Publishing Ltd.
Livery Place
35 Livery Street
Birmingham
B3 2PB, UK.
ISBN 978-1-78712-994-8

www.packtpub.com

Credits

Author

Jon Hoffman

Reviewer

Andrea Prearo

Commissioning Editor

Ashwin Nair

Acquisition Editor

Smeet Thakkar

Content Development Editor

Sumeet Sawant

Technical Editor

Egan Lobo

Copy Editor

Safis Editing

Project Coordinator

Shweta H Birwatkar

Proofreader

Safis Editing

Indexer

Aishwarya Gangawane

Graphics

Disha Haria

Production Coordinator

Nilesh Mohite

About the Author

Jon Hoffman has over 20 years of experience in the field of information technology. Over those 20 years, Jon has worked in the areas of system administration, network administration, network security, application development, and architecture. Currently, Jon works as a senior software engineer for Syn-Tech Systems.

Jon has developed extensively for the iOS platform since 2008. This includes several apps that he has published in the App Store, apps that he has written for third parties, and numerous enterprise applications. What really drives Jon is the challenges the information technology field provides and there is nothing more exhilarating to him than overcoming a challenge.

You can follow Jon on his two blogs: `http://masteringswift.blogspot.com` and `http://myroboticadventure.blogspot.com`.

Some of Jon's other interests are watching baseball (Go Sox) and basketball (Go Celtics). Jon also really enjoys Tae Kwon Do where he and his oldest daughter Kailey earned their black belts together early in 2014, Kim (his wife) earned her black belt in December 2014, and his youngest daughter is currently working towards her black belt.

I would like to thank my wonderful wife, Kim, without whose support, encouragement, patience, and understanding, this book would have never been written. I would also like to thank my two wonderful daughters, Kailey and Kara, who have both been my inspiration and driving force since the days they were born.

About the Reviewer

Andrea Prearo is a software engineer with over 15 years of experience.

He is originally from Italy, and after a decade of writing software in C/C++ and C#, he moved to the Bay Area in 2011 to start developing mobile apps.

In the last few years, he has been focusing on Swift, Objective-C, iOS, and microservices, with some short explorations of the Android platform.

Currently, he is a member of the iOS development team at Capital One, working on the company's flagship mobile banking app.

His interests include reading books, watching movies, and hiking. From time to time, he also blogs about tech on Medium: `https://medium.com/@andrea.prearo`.

I would like to thank my wonderful wife, Nicole, for her never-ending support in all my endeavors.

www.PacktPub.com

For support files and downloads related to your book, please visit `www.PacktPub.com`.

Did you know that Packt offers eBook versions of every book published, with PDF and ePub files available? You can upgrade to the eBook version at `www.PacktPub.com` and as a print book customer, you are entitled to a discount on the eBook copy. Get in touch with us at `service@packtpub.com` for more details.

At `www.PacktPub.com`, you can also read a collection of free technical articles, sign up for a range of free newsletters and receive exclusive discounts and offers on Packt books and eBooks.

`https://www.packtpub.com/mapt`

Get the most in-demand software skills with Mapt. Mapt gives you full access to all Packt books and video courses, as well as industry-leading tools to help you plan your personal development and advance your career.

Why subscribe?

- Fully searchable across every book published by Packt
- Copy and paste, print, and bookmark content
- On demand and accessible via a web browser

Table of Contents

Preface

This book is about protocol-oriented programming. When Apple announced Swift 2 at the **World Wide Developers Conference (WWDC)** in 2015 they also declared that Swift was the world's first protocol-oriented programming language. From its name, we may assume that protocol-oriented programming is all about the protocol; however, that would be an incorrect assumption. Protocol-oriented programming is about so much more than just the protocol; it is actually a new way of not only writing applications but also how we think about programming.

One of the biggest misconceptions about protocol-oriented programming is that it is just another name for object-oriented programming. Chapter 1, *Object-Oriented Programming and Protocol-Oriented Programming*, immediately takes on this myth by comparing protocol-oriented programming to object-oriented programming to see what is similar and what is different. We also discuss the advantages and disadvantages of both programming paradigms.

In chapters two to six, we take an in-depth look at each of the components of the protocol-oriented programming paradigm. These chapters are designed to give the reader a solid understanding of the different components of protocol-oriented programming so they will understand how they can use these components in their applications.

The last two chapters are written to help the reader understand how they can design their application in a protocol-oriented programming way. Chapter 7, *Adopting Design Patterns in Swift*, looks at how we would implement several design patterns in a protocol-oriented way and Chapter 8, *Case Studies*, looks at three real-world case studies to reinforce everything previously discussed in the book.

What this book covers

Chapter 1, *Object-Oriented Programming and Protocol-Oriented Programming*, will show the differences between object-oriented programming and protocol-oriented programming giving the reader a good understanding of the difference paradigms. By the end of the chapter, the reader should have a basic understanding of protocol-oriented programming and what it offers.

Chapter 2, *Our Type Choices*, will look at the different types that Swift offers (structs, classes, enums, and tuples). We will show several examples of when to use the various types and when not too.

Chapter 3, *Catching Our Errors*, will look at the various ways that we can catch and report errors. This chapter will not only cover the new Swift 2 do-try-catch blocks but also the older error catching patterns.

Chapter 4, *All About the Protocol*, will be all about the protocol. We will show the advantages of using protocols and why, in our design, we should always think about the protocol first and the actual types that conform to the protocol second.

Chapter 5, *Let's Extend Some Types*, will cover extensions in great detail. We will look at how to extend standard Swift types such as structures and classes. We will also look at protocol extensions and discuss why they are so important to protocol-oriented programming.

Chapter 6, *Working with Generics*, will cover generics. We will look at how generics can be used with the protocol-oriented programming paradigm to write flexible and reusable code.

Chapter 7, *Adopting Design Patterns in Swift*, will implement several design patterns using protocol-oriented programming. For each of the design patterns, we will look at the problem they are designed to solve and how to implement the pattern.

Chapter 8, *Case Studies*, will explore three case studies. This chapter is designed to pull everything from the first six chapters together to show the reader how to use protocol-oriented programming in real-world situations.

What you need for this book

To follow along with the examples in this book, the reader will need to have an Apple computer with OS X 10.12 or higher installed. They will also need to install Xcode version 8.0 or higher with Swift version 3 or higher. At least a basic knowledge of the Swift programming language is required.

Who this book is for

This book is intended for the developer that has at least an introductory knowledge of the Swift programming language and wants to understand what protocol-oriented programming is. This book is written for the developer who not only wants to understand protocol-oriented but also wants to fully understand the different components of the programming paradigm. This book is written for the developer who learns best by looking at and working with code, because every concept covered in the book is backed by example code written to give the reader a solid understanding of the current topic and to demonstrate how to properly implement it.

Conventions

In this book, you will find a number of text styles that distinguish between different kinds of information. Here are some examples of these styles and an explanation of their meaning.

Code words in text, database table names, folder names, filenames, file extensions, pathnames, dummy URLs, user input, and Twitter handles are shown as follows: "We will start forming our object-oriented design by creating a `TerrainType` enumeration that will be used to define the different vehicle, attack, and movement types."

A block of code is set as follows:

```
enum TerrainType {
    case Land
    case Sea
    case Air
}
```

New terms and **important words** are shown in bold. Words that you see on the screen, for example, in menus or dialog boxes, appear in the text like this: "From this menu, we will want to select the **Create a new Xcode project** option."

Warnings or important notes appear in a box like this.

Tips and tricks appear like this.

Reader feedback

Feedback from our readers is always welcome. Let us know what you think about this book-what you liked or disliked. Reader feedback is important for us as it helps us develop titles that you will really get the most out of.

To send us general feedback, simply e-mail feedback@packtpub.com, and mention the book's title in the subject of your message.

If there is a topic that you have expertise in and you are interested in either writing or contributing to a book, see our author guide at www.packtpub.com/authors.

Customer support

Now that you are the proud owner of a Packt book, we have a number of things to help you to get the most from your purchase.

Downloading the example code

You can download the example code files for this book from your account at http://www.packtpub.com. If you purchased this book elsewhere, you can visit http://www.packtpub.com/support and register to have the files e-mailed directly to you.

You can download the code files by following these steps:

1. Log in or register to our website using your e-mail address and password.
2. Hover the mouse pointer on the **SUPPORT** tab at the top.
3. Click on **Code Downloads & Errata**.
4. Enter the name of the book in the **Search** box.
5. Select the book for which you're looking to download the code files.
6. Choose from the drop-down menu where you purchased this book from.
7. Click on **Code Download**.

Once the file is downloaded, please make sure that you unzip or extract the folder using the latest version of:

- WinRAR / 7-Zip for Windows
- Zipeg / iZip / UnRarX for Mac
- 7-Zip / PeaZip for Linux

The code bundle for the book is also hosted on GitHub at `https://github.com/PacktPubl ishing/Swift-3-Protocol-Oriented-Programming-Second-Edition`. We also have other code bundles from our rich catalog of books and videos available at `https://github.com/P acktPublishing/`. Check them out!

Downloading the color images of this book

We also provide you with a PDF file that has color images of the screenshots/diagrams used in this book. The color images will help you better understand the changes in the output. You can download this file from `https://www.packtpub.com/sites/default/files/down loads/Swift3ProtocolOrientedProgrammingSecondEdition_ColorImages.pdf`.

Errata

Although we have taken every care to ensure the accuracy of our content, mistakes do happen. If you find a mistake in one of our books-maybe a mistake in the text or the code-we would be grateful if you could report this to us. By doing so, you can save other readers from frustration and help us improve subsequent versions of this book. If you find any errata, please report them by visiting `http://www.packtpub.com/submit-errata`, selecting your book, clicking on the **Errata Submission Form** link, and entering the details of your errata. Once your errata are verified, your submission will be accepted and the errata will be uploaded to our website or added to any list of existing errata under the Errata section of that title.

To view the previously submitted errata, go to `https://www.packtpub.com/books/conten t/support` and enter the name of the book in the search field. The required information will appear under the **Errata** section.

Piracy

Piracy of copyrighted material on the Internet is an ongoing problem across all media. At Packt, we take the protection of our copyright and licenses very seriously. If you come across any illegal copies of our works in any form on the Internet, please provide us with the location address or website name immediately so that we can pursue a remedy.

Please contact us at copyright@packtpub.com with a link to the suspected pirated material.

We appreciate your help in protecting our authors and our ability to bring you valuable content.

Questions

If you have a problem with any aspect of this book, you can contact us at questions@packtpub.com, and we will do our best to address the problem.

1
Object-Oriented and Protocol-Oriented Programming

This book is about protocol-oriented programming. When Apple announced Swift 2 at the **World Wide Developers Conference (WWDC)** in 2015, they also declared that Swift was the world's first protocol-oriented programming language. From its name, we may assume that protocol-oriented programming is all about the protocol; however, this would be a wrong assumption. Protocol-oriented programming is about so much more than just the protocol; it is actually a new way of not only writing applications, but also how we think about programming.

In this chapter, you will learn the following:

- How Swift can be used as an object-oriented programming language
- How Swift can be used as a protocol-oriented programming language
- The differences between object-oriented programming and protocol-oriented programming
- The advantages that protocol-oriented programming has over object-oriented programming

While this book is about protocol-oriented programming, we are going to start off by discussing how Swift can be used as an object-oriented programming language. Having a good understanding of object-oriented programming will help us understand protocol-oriented programming and also give us some insight into the issues protocol-oriented programming is designed to solve.

What is object-oriented programming?

Object-oriented programming is a design philosophy. Writing applications with an object-oriented programming language is fundamentally different than writing applications with older procedural languages, such as C and Pascal. Procedural languages use a set of instructions to tell the computer what to do step-by-step by relying on procedures (or routines). Object-oriented programming, however, is all about the object. This may seem like a pretty obvious statement given the name but essentially, when we think about object-oriented programming, we need to think about the object.

The object is a data structure that contains information about the attributes of the object, in the form of properties, and the actions performed by or to the object, in the form of methods. Objects can be considered things and in the English language they would normally be considered nouns. These objects can be real-world or virtual objects. If you take a look around, you will see many real-world objects and, virtually all of them can be modeled in an object-oriented way with attributes and actions.

As I am writing this chapter, I look outside and see a lake, numerous trees, grass, my dog, and the fence in our backyard. All of these items can be modeled as objects with both properties and actions.

I am also thinking about one of my all-time favorite energy drinks. That energy drink is called Jolt. I'm not sure how many people remember Jolt, but I would not have made it through college without it. A can of Jolt can be modeled as an object with attributes (volume, quantity of caffeine, temperature, and size) and actions (drinking and temperature change).

We could keep the cans of Jolt in a cooler to keep them cold. This cooler could also be modeled as an object because it has attributes (temperature, cans of Jolt, and maximum number of cans) and actions (adding and removing cans).

The object is what makes object-oriented programming so powerful. With an object, we can model real-world items, such as a can of Jolt, or virtual objects, such as characters in a video game. These objects can then interact within our application to model real-world behavior or the behavior we want in our virtual world.

Within a computer application, we cannot create an object without a blueprint that tells the application what properties and actions to expect from the object. In most object-oriented languages, this blueprint comes in the form of a class. A class is a construct that allows us to encapsulate the properties and actions of an object into a single type that models the entity we are trying to represent in our code.

We use initializers within our classes to create instances of the class. We usually use these initializers to set the initial values of the properties for the object, or to perform any other initialization that our class needs. Once we create the instance of a class, we can then use it within our code.

All of this explanation about object-oriented programming is fine, but nothing demonstrates the concepts better than the actual code. Before we can begin coding we will need to define the requirements. In this chapter, we will show how we could design vehicle types for a video game in both an object-oriented and a protocol-oriented way. Let's look at the requirements for the vehicle types.

Requirements for the sample code

When we develop applications we usually have a set of requirements that we need to work towards. Our sample projects in this chapter are no different. The following is a list of requirements for the vehicle types that we will be creating:

- We will have three categories of vehicle: Sea, land, and air
- A vehicle can be a member of multiple categories
- Vehicles may move or attack when they are on a tile that matches any of the categories they are in
- Vehicles will be unable to move to or attack on a tile that does not match any of the categories they are in
- When a vehicle's hit points reach 0, the vehicle will be considered incapacitated
- We will need to keep all active vehicles in a single array that we can loop through

For our projects in this chapter, we will be demonstrating the design with only a few vehicles, but we know that the number of vehicle types will grow as we develop the game. In this chapter, we will not be implementing a lot of the logic for the vehicles because our focus is the design and not the code that makes the vehicles move and attack.

Let's start off by looking at how we would design these vehicles in an object-oriented way, and how Swift functions as an object-oriented programming language.

Swift as an object-oriented programming language

Swift provides full support for developing applications in an object-oriented way. Actually, prior to Swift 2, I considered Swift primarily an object-oriented language in the same way that I considered Java and C# to be object-oriented languages. In this section, we will be designing the vehicle types in an object-oriented way and seeing the drawbacks of this design.

Before we look at the code, let's create a very basic class diagram that shows how we would design the vehicle class hierarchy for an object-oriented design. I usually start off by doing a very basic diagram that simply shows the classes themselves without much detail. This helps me picture the class hierarchy in my mind. The following diagram shows the class hierarchy for the object-oriented design:

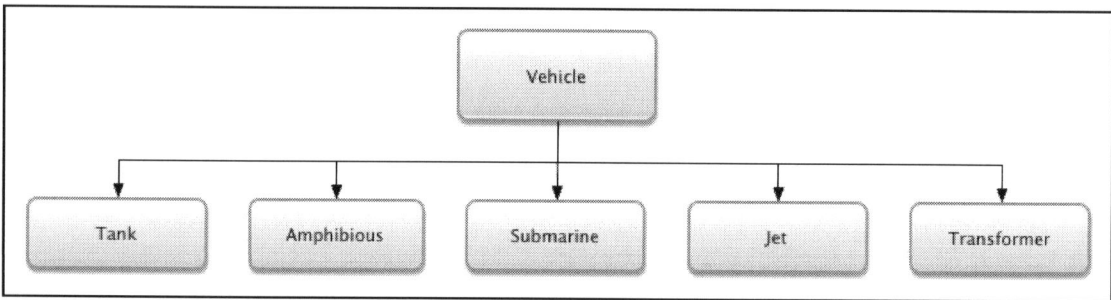

This diagram shows that we have one superclass named `Vehicle` and five subclasses named `Tank`, `Amphibious`, `Submarine`, `Jet`, and `Transformer`. With a class hierarchy, each of the subclasses will inherit all of the properties and methods from the superclass therefore, any common code and properties can be implemented in the `Vehicle` superclass and all of the subclasses will inherit them.

We may think that, with the three categories (land, air, and sea) in our requirements, we would want to create a larger class hierarchy where the middle layer would contain separate superclasses for land, air, and sea vehicles. This would allow us to separate the code for each category into its own superclass; however, that is not possible with the requirements. The reason this is not possible is that the vehicle types may be members of multiple categories and with a single inheritance language such as Swift, each class can have one and only one superclass. This means that if we created separate land and sea superclasses, for example, then the `Amphibious` class could be a subclass of either the land or the sea type but not both.

Since Swift is a single inheritance language, and we can have only one superclass for the vehicle classes, that superclass will need to contain the code required for each of the three categories. Having a single superclass such as this is one of the drawbacks of object-oriented design because the superclass can become very bloated.

We will start forming our object-oriented design by creating a TerrainType enumeration that will be used to define the different vehicle, attack, and movement types. The TerrainType enumeration is defined like this:

```
enum TerrainType {
    case Land
    case Sea
    case Air
}
```

Now let's looks at how we would define the Vehicle superclass and the properties within this class:

```
class Vehicle {
    fileprivate var vehicleTypes = [TerrainType]()
    fileprivate var vehicleAttackTypes = [TerrainType]()
    fileprivate var vehicleMovementTypes = [TerrainType]()
    fileprivate var landAttackRange = -1
    fileprivate var seaAttackRange = -1
    fileprivate var airAttackRange = -1
    fileprivate var hitPoints = 0
}
```

We start the Vehicle type off by defining seven properties. The first three properties are arrays of the TerrainType type. These three arrays will keep track of the vehicle type (vehicleTypes array), the types of terrain the vehicle can attack from (vehicleAttackTypes array), and the types of terrain the vehicle can move to (vehicleMovementTypes array).

The next three properties (landAttackRange, seaAttackRange, and airAttackRange integers) will contain the attack range of the vehicle for each of the different terrain types. Finally, the last property will keep track of the hit points of the vehicle.

The preference is for each of these properties, except for the hitPoints property, to be constants however, a subclass cannot set/change the value of a constant defined in a superclass. This means that we will need to rely on Swift's access control functionality to control the access to these properties.

We defined the properties as `fileprivate` variables because we need to set them from the subclasses however, we do not want external entities to change them. This access control was introduced in Swift 3, and allows access to the properties and methods from any code within the same source file that the item is defined in. In order for this to work, the subclass needs to be defined in the same physical file as the superclass, which is definitely not the ideal solution because this file could get very large. However, in this object-oriented design, it is the best option that we have to prevent these properties from being changed by instances of other types.

Since the properties are marked as `fileprivate`, we will need to create some getter methods that will retrieve the values of the properties. We will also create methods to see what types of terrain the vehicle can attack from and move to. Let's look at these methods:

```
func isVehicleType(type: TerrainType) -> Bool {
    return vehicleTypes.contains(type)
}
func canVehicleAttack(type: TerrainType) -> Bool {
    return vehicleAttackTypes.contains(type)
}
func canVehicleMove(type: TerrainType) -> Bool {
    return vehicleMovementTypes.contains(type)
}
func doLandAttack() {}
func doLandMovement() {}
func doSeaAttack() {}
func doSeaMovement() {}
func doAirAttack() {}
func doAirMovement() {}
func takeHit(amount: Int) { hitPoints -= amount }
func hitPointsRemaining() -> Int { return hitPoints }
func isAlive() -> Bool { return hitPoints > 0 ? true : false }
```

The first method (`isVehicleType` method) accepts one parameter of the `TerrainType` type and will return true if the `vehicleTypes` array contains that terrain type. This will allow the external code to see if the vehicle is of a certain type. The next two methods also accept a parameter of the `TerrainType` type and will return true if the `vehicleAttackTypes` or `vehicleMovementTypes` arrays contain that terrain type. These two methods would be used to see whether a vehicle can move to or attack from a certain type of terrain.

The next six methods will define the attacks or movement for the different terrains. We will also look at a couple of additional methods that will see if the vehicle is alive, and deduct hit points when the vehicle takes a hit.

One big disadvantage to this design, as we noted earlier, is that all of the subclasses need to be in the same physical file as the Vehicle superclass. Given how large the vehicle classes can be, we probably don't want them all in the same source file. To avoid this, we could set the property's access controls to internal or public, but that would not prevent the properties from being changed by instances of other types. This is a major drawback of object-oriented design.

Another disadvantage of the object-oriented design is that we need to provide methods so the vehicle can attack from and move to each of the different terrain types, even though most vehicles will not be able to attack from and move to all of the different terrain types. Even though there is no code in the method implementations, the external code can still call any of the attack or movement methods. For example, even though our Submarine type is going to be a sea-only type, the external code will be able to call the movement and attack methods for land and air types. Superclasses that are bloated, such as this, are a major disadvantage of single-inheritance, object-oriented programming languages such as Swift.

 In this example, we are only defining a very small subset of the functionality that would be needed for our vehicle types in a video game. Imagine how big the Vehicle superclass could be if all of the functionality was being implemented.

Let's take a look at how we would subclass the Vehicle class by seeing how we would create the Tank, Amphibious, and Transformer classes. We will start with the Tank class:

```
class Tank: Vehicle {
    override init() {
        super.init()
        vehicleTypes = [.Land]
        vehicleAttackTypes = [.Land]
        vehicleMovementTypes = [.Land]
        landAttackRange = 5

        hitPoints = 68
    }
    override func doLandAttack() { print("Tank Attack") }
    override func doLandMovement() { print("Tank Move") }
}
```

The `Tank` class is a subclass of the `Vehicle` class, and we begin this class by overriding the default initializer. In the initializer, we set several inherited properties. Not how we add the `Land` value, the `vehicleTypes`, `vehicleAttackTypes`, and `vehicleMovementTypes` arrays. This specifies that the `Tank` type is a land vehicle and can attack from and move to land tiles. Using arrays to keep track of the type of vehicle the class is and the types of terrain the vehicle can move to and attack from is another disadvantage of the object-oriented design. Even for the most experienced developer, it is very easy to enter the wrong value into the arrays causing unexpected behavior.

In the `Tank` class, we also override the `doLandAttack()` and `doLandMovement()` methods from the `Vehicle` superclass since the `TankTank` class is a land vehicle. We do not override the other attack and movement methods from the `Vehicle` superclass because the tank should not be moving to or attacking from the sea or air terrains. Even though we do not override these methods, they are still a part of the `Tank` class because they are inherited from the `Vehicle` superclass, and there isn't any way to prevent external code from calling these methods. This is another disadvantage of object-oriented design.

Now let's look at the `Amphibious` and `Transformer` classes. These classes are very similar to the `Tank` class, except they can move to and attack from multiple terrain types. Here is the `Amphibious` class that can move and attack on both land and sea terrains:

```
class Amphibious: Vehicle {
    override init() {
        super.init()
        vehicleTypes = [.Land, .Sea]
        vehicleAttackTypes = [.Land, .Sea]
        vehicleMovementTypes = [.Land, .Sea]
        landAttackRange = 1
        seaAttackRange = 1
        hitPoints = 25
    }
    override func doLandAttack() {
        print("Amphibious Land Attack")
    }
    override func doLandMovement() {
        print("Amphibious Land Move")
    }
    override func doSeaAttack() {
        print("Amphibious Sea Attack")
    }
    override func doSeaMovement() {
        print("Amphibious Sea Move")
    }
}
```

Now let's see the `Transformer` class that can move to and attack from all three terrain types:

```
class Transformer: Vehicle {
    override init() {
        super.init()
        vehicleTypes = [.Land, .Sea, .Air]
        vehicleAttackTypes = [.Land, .Sea, .Air]
        vehicleMovementTypes = [.Land, .Sea, .Air]
        landAttackRange = 7
        seaAttackRange = 10
        airAttackRange = 12
        hitPoints = 75
    }
    override func doLandAttack() {
        print("Transformer Land Attack")
    }
    override func doLandMovement() {
        print("Transformer Land Move")
    }
    override func doSeaAttack() {
        print("Transformer Sea Attack")
    }
    override func doSeaMovement() {
        print("Transformer Sea Move")
    }
    override func doAirAttack() {
        print("Transformer Air Attack")
    }
    override func doAirMovement() {
        print("Transformer Air Move")
    }
}
```

Now that we have created the vehicle types, let's take a look at how we would use them. One of the original requirements was to be able to keep instances of all the vehicle types in a single array. This will allow us to loop through all active vehicles and perform any actions needed. For this we will use polymorphism.

Polymorphism comes from the Greek words *poly* (for many) and *morph* (for forms). In computer science, we use polymorphism when we want to use a single interface to represent multiple types within our code. Polymorphism gives us the ability to interact with multiple types in a uniform manner. With object-oriented programming languages, we can achieve polymorphism through subclassing, where we interact with the various subclasses using the interface provided by the superclass.

Let's see how we would use polymorphism to keep all instances of the various vehicle types in a single array and interact with them. Since all of the vehicle types are subclasses of the `Vehicle` superclass, we can create an array of vehicle types, and store instances of any type that is a subclass of the `Vehicle` superclass, as shown here:

```
var vehicles = [Vehicle]()

var vh1 = Amphibious()
var vh2 = Amphibious()
var vh3 = Tank()
var vh4 = Transformer()

vehicles.append(vh1)
vehicles.append(vh2)
vehicles.append(vh3)
vehicles.append(vh4)
```

Now that we have an array of vehicle types, we can interact with each instance through the interface presented by the vehicle type. The following code illustrates this:

```
for (index, vehicle) in vehicles.enumerated() {
    if vehicle.isVehicleType(type: .Air) {
        print("Vehicle at \(index) is Air")
        if vehicle.canVehicleAttack(type: .Air) {
            print("---Can do Air attack")
        }
        if vehicle.canVehicleMove(type: .Air) {
            print("---Can do Air movement")
        }
    }
    if vehicle.isVehicleType(type: .Land){
        print("Vehicle at \(index) is Land")
        if vehicle.canVehicleAttack(type: .Land) {
            print("---Can do Land attack")
        }
        if vehicle.canVehicleMove(type: .Land) {
            print("---Can do Land movement")
        }
    }
    if vehicle.isVehicleType(type: .Sea) {
        print("Vehicle at \(index) is Sea")
        if vehicle.canVehicleAttack(type: .Sea) {
            print("---Can do Sea attack")
        }
        if vehicle.canVehicleMove(type: .Sea) {
            print("---Can do Sea movement")
        }
```

```
        }
    }
```

In this code, we loop through the `vehicles` array and use the `isVehicleType(type:)` method to determine if the vehicle is of a certain type, and then call the appropriate movement and attack methods. Note that we do not use an `if-else` or a `switch` statement here because any vehicle may be a member of multiple types, and we want to recheck the type, even if the vehicle matched a previous type.

This code works pretty well, but, as we will see in the *protocol-oriented design* section, we can make the code a lot cleaner, safer, and easier to read.

Before we look at the protocol-oriented design, let's review the drawbacks of object-oriented design that we pointed out in this section.

Drawbacks to object-oriented design

As we went through our object-oriented design, we pointed out several issues with such an approach. In this section, we will review these issues so we understand how protocol-oriented design addresses them.

Two of the drawbacks that we saw are directly related to each other, and are the result of Swift being a single-inheritance language. An object-oriented design with a single-inheritance language, such as Swift, can lead to bloated superclasses because we may need to include functionality that is needed by only a few of the subclasses. This leads to the second drawback related to Swift being a single-inheritance language, which is the inheritance of functionality that a type does not need.

Another drawback in our design is we could not create constants in our superclass that can be set by the subclasses. In our design, there were several properties that we would like to set in the initializer of our subclasses and then never change. It would be ideal if we could make these constants; however, a constant defined in one class cannot be set in a subclass of that type.

The final drawback that we saw was the inability to set a property or method to be accessible only by subclasses of that type. To get around this, we used the `fileprivate` access control to say that only code defined in the same source file could access the properties however, this workaround is not an ideal solution because we may not want to put all of the subclasses in the same source file as the superclass.

Now that we have looked at the object-oriented design, let's redesign our vehicle types in a protocol-oriented way.

Swift as a protocol-oriented programming language

As we did with the object-oriented design, let's start off by creating a very basic diagram that shows how we would design the vehicle types in a protocol-oriented way. Just like the object-oriented diagram, this will be a very basic diagram that simply shows the types themselves without much detail:

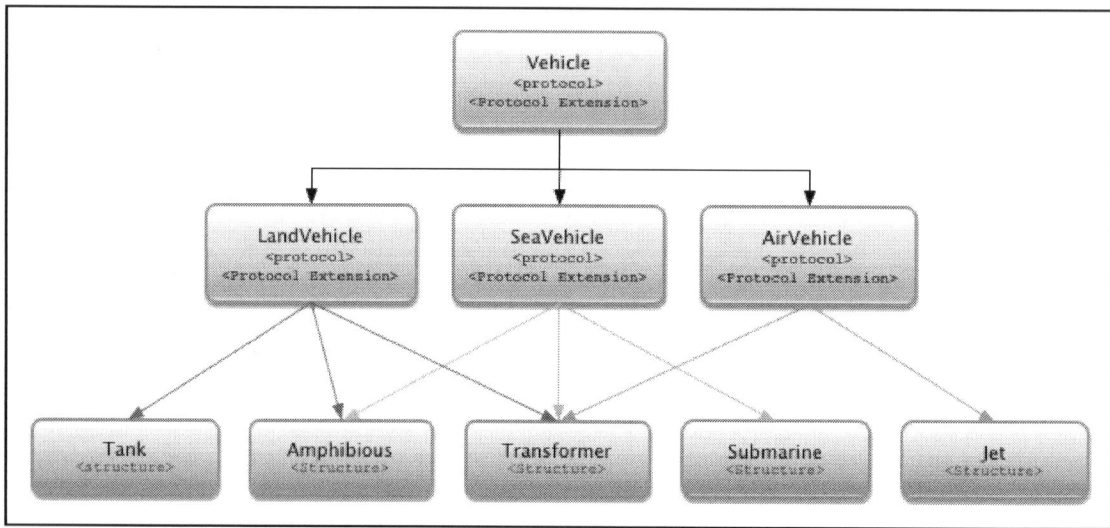

As we can see, the protocol-oriented design is quite a bit different from the object-oriented design. In our object-oriented design, we started the design with the superclass which became the focus of the design, since all of the subclasses inherited the functionality and properties from this superclass.

In the protocol-oriented design, we start the design with the protocol. The protocols and protocol extensions are also the focus of the protocol-oriented design however, as we will see throughout this book, the protocol-oriented design is about so much more than just the protocol.

In this new design, we use three techniques that make protocol-oriented programming significantly different from object-oriented programming. These techniques are protocol inheritance, protocol composition, and protocol extensions.

Protocol inheritance is where one protocol can inherit the requirements from one or more other protocols. This is similar to class inheritance in object-oriented programming however, instead of inheriting functionality we are inheriting requirements. One advantage that protocol inheritance has over class inheritance in Swift is that protocols can inherit the requirements from multiple protocols. In our example, the LandVehicle, SeaVehicle, and AirVehicle protocols inherit the requirements from the Vehicle protocol.

Protocol composition allows types to conform to more than one protocol. In our example, there are some types (Tank, Submarine, and Jet structures) that conform to a single protocol; however there are also two types (Amphibious and Transformer structures) that take advantage of protocol composition by conforming to multiple protocols.

Protocol inheritance and composition are extremely important to protocol-oriented design because they allow us to create smaller and more specific protocols. This allows us to avoid the bloated superclass that we may end up getting with object-oriented designs. We do need to be careful not to create protocols that are too granular because they will become hard to maintain and manage.

Protocol extensions allow us to extend a protocol to provide method and property implementations to conforming types. This gives us the ability to provide common implementations to all the conforming types, eliminating the need to provide an implementation in each individual type or the need to create a class hierarchy. While protocol extensions may not seem too exciting, once you see how powerful they really are, they will transform the way you think about application design.

We will cover these techniques in much greater detail in later chapters. For now, just knowing what these techniques are will help us understand the basics of our design. Let's begin our implementation by creating the Vehicle protocol. The Vehicle protocol, for our example, will define a single property name hitPoints that will keep track of the vehicle's remaining hit points:

```
protocol Vehicle {
    var hitPoints: Int {get set}
}
```

If you recall from our object-oriented design, we had three methods defined as takeHit(amount:), hitPointsRemaining(), and isAlive(). The implementation for these methods would be the same for every vehicle type, which makes them great candidates to be implemented in a protocol extension. The following code shows how we would create a Vehicle protocol extension, and how we would implement these three methods within the extension:

```
extension Vehicle {
```

```
    mutating func takeHit(amount: Int) { hitPoints -= amount }
    func hitPointsRemaining() -> Int { return hitPoints }
    func isAlive() -> Bool { return hitPoints > 0 ? true : false }
}
```

Now, any type that conforms to the `Vehicle` protocol, or any type that conforms to a protocol that inherits from the `Vehicle` protocol, will automatically receive these methods. It is important to note that protocols that inherit requirements from another protocol also inherit the functionality provided by the protocol's extensions as well.

Now let's take a look at how we would define the `LandVehicle`, `SeaVehicle`, and `AirVehicle` protocols:

```
protocol LandVehicle: Vehicle {
    var landAttack: Bool {get}
    var landMovement: Bool {get}
    var landAttackRange: Int {get}
    func doLandAttack()
    func doLandMovement()
}

protocol SeaVehicle: Vehicle {
    var seaAttack: Bool {get}
    var seaMovement: Bool {get}
    var seaAttackRange: Int {get}
    func doSeaAttack()
    func doSeaMovement()
}

protocol AirVehicle: Vehicle {
    var airAttack: Bool {get}
    var airMovement: Bool {get}
    var airAttackRange: Int {get}
    func doAirAttack()
    func doAirMovement()
}
```

There are a couple of things to note about these protocols. The first is they all inherit the requirements from the `Vehicle` protocol, which also means they inherit the functionality from the `Vehicle` protocol extension.

Another thing to note about these protocols is that they only contain the requirements needed for their particular type of vehicle. If you recall, the Vehicle superclass from our object-oriented design contained the requirements for all vehicle types. Dividing the requirements up into three separate protocols makes the code much safer, and easier to maintain and manage. If we do need some common functionality we can add a protocol extension to any or all of the protocols.

We defined the properties for these protocols with only the get attribute, which means we will be defining the properties as constants within the types that conform to these protocols. This is a really big advantage in using protocol-oriented design because it prevents code from changing the values once they are set, introducing errors that are hard to trace.

Now let's look at how we can create types that conform to these protocols. We will create the Tank, Amphibious, and Transformer types (as we did in our object-oriented design) starting with the Tank type:

```
struct Tank: LandVehicle {
    var hitPoints = 68
    let landAttackRange = 5
    let landAttack = true
    let landMovement = true
    func doLandAttack() { print("Tank Attack") }
    func doLandMovement() { print("Tank Move") }
}
```

There are several differences between the Tank type defined here and the Tank type defined in our object-oriented design. In order to see these differences, let's look at the Tank type that was defined in our object-oriented design:

```
class Tank: Vehicle {
    override init() {
        super.init()
        vehicleTypes = [.Land]
        vehicleAttackTypes = [.Land]
        vehicleMovementTypes = [.Land]
        landAttackRange = 5

        hitPoints = 68
    }
    override func doLandAttack() { print("Tank Attack") }
    override func doLandMovement() { print("Tank Move") }
}
```

The first thing that we can see is that the `Tank` type from our object-oriented design is a class, which is a reference type, while the `Tank` type defined in this section is a structure, which is a value type. We could have defined the Tank type as a class but using a structure has some advantages. We will discuss the different type choices in depth in `Chapter 2`, *Our Type Choices*.

The big differences between the two types is that in the `Tank` type defined in this section is we are able to use the default initializer that the structure provides, and we define the properties as constants; therefore, they can't be changed once they are set. In the `Tank` type from our object-oriented design, we had to override the initializer and then set the properties within the initializer. The properties in the object-oriented design were also variables, which may be changed once they are set.

One thing that we do not see when we look at the two `Tank` types is that the `Tank` type from the protocol-oriented design contains only the functionality for land vehicles. The `Tank` type from the object-oriented design inherits the functionality and properties for the sea and air types from the `Vehicle` superclass, even though it does not need that functionality.

Now let's see how we would create the `Amphibious` and `Transformer` types:

```
struct Amphibious: LandVehicle, SeaVehicle {
    var hitPoints = 25
    let landAttackRange = 1
    let seaAttackRange = 1
    let landAttack = true
    let landMovement = true
    let seaAttackRange = 1
    let seaAttack = true
    let seaMovement = true
    func doLandAttack() { print("Amphibious Land Attack") }
    func doLandMovement() { print("Amphibious Land Move") }
    func doSeaAttack() { print("Amphibious Sea Attack") }
    func doSeaMovement() { print("Amphibious Sea Move") }
}
struct Transformer: LandVehicle, SeaVehicle, AirVehicle {
    var hitPoints = 75
    let landAttackRange = 7
    let landAttack = true
    let landMovement = true
    let seaAttack = true
    let seaMovement = true
    let airAttack = true
    let airMovement = true
    func doLandAttack() { print("Transformer Land Attack") }
```

```
        func doLandMovement() { print("Transformer Land Move") }
        func doSeaAttack() { print("Transformer Sea Attack") }
        func doSeaMovement() { print("Transformer Sea Move") }
        func doAirAttack() { print("Transformer Sea Attack") }
        func doAirMovement() { print("Transformer Sea Move") }
}
```

We can see that the Amphibious and Transformer types are very similar to the Tank type, however they use protocol composition to conform to multiple vehicle types. This allows, for example, the Amphibious type to contain the functionality for both land and sea vehicles.

Now let's see how we would use these new types. As with our object-oriented design, we have the requirement to be able to keep instances of all of the vehicle types in a single array. This allows us to loop through all active vehicles and perform any actions needed. For this, we will use polymorphism just as we did with our object-oriented design however with our protocol-oriented design, we will use the requirements provided by the protocols to interact with the instances of the vehicle types. Let's see how we would do this by creating an array and putting several instances of the vehicle types into it:

```
var vehicles = [Vehicle]()

var vh1 = Amphibious()
var vh2 = Amphibious()
var vh3 = Tank()
var vh4 = Transformer()

vehicles.append(vh1)
vehicles.append(vh2)
vehicles.append(vh3)
vehicles.append(vh4)
```

This code looks exactly like the code from our object-oriented design. In this code, we create an array that will store instances of types that conform to the Vehicle type. With protocol inheritance, this means the array will also accept types that conform to protocols that inherit the Vehicle protocol. In our example, this means that the array will accept instances of types that conform to the LandVehicle, SeaVehicle, AirVehicle, and Vehicle protocols.

The array, in this example, is defined to contain instances of types that conform to the `Vehicle` protocol. This means that we can use the interface defined by the `Vehicle` protocol to interact with the types in the array. Looking at the `Vehicle` protocol, that really is not very useful however, we can use another really nice feature in the Swift language to help us. This feature is pattern matching, and in our case, we will be using the type-casting pattern. The type-casting pattern matches a value if the type at runtime is the same as the type specified. Let's see how this works:

```
for (index, vehicle) in vehicles.enumerated() {
    if let Vehicle = vehicle as? AirVehicle {
        print("Vehicle at \(index) is Air")
    }
    if let Vehicle = vehicle as? LandVehicle {
        print("Vehicle at \(index) is Land")
    }
    if let Vehicle = vehicle as? SeaVehicle {
        print("Vehicle at \(index) is Sea")
    }
}
```

In this code, we use a `for` loop statement to loop through the `vehicles` array. We use an `as?` type-casting pattern to see if the instances conform to the various protocols (`AirVehicle`, `LandVehicle`, and `SeaVehicle` protocols), and if so, we print out a message.

Accessing the vehicle types in this manner is very similar to how we accessed them in the object-oriented example however, what if we only wanted to get one type of vehicle rather than all vehicles? We are able to do this with another type-casting pattern with the `where` keyword. The following example shows how to do this:

```
for (index, vehicle) in vehicles.enumerated()
    where vehicle LandVehicle {
    var vh = vehicle as! LandVehicle
    if vh.landAttack {
        print("---Can do Land attack")
    }
    if vh.landMovement {
        print("---Can do Land movement")
    }
}
```

In this example, we use the `where` keyword to filter the results of the `for` loop to retrieve only instances that conform to the `LandVehicle` protocol. We can then typecast any instance that is returned from the `for` loop as an instance that conforms to the `LandVehicle` protocol and interact with it using the interface provided by the protocol.

Now that we have finished redesigning, let's summarize what protocol-oriented programming is and how it is different from object-oriented programming.

Summarizing protocol-oriented programming and object-oriented programming

We just saw how Swift can be used as both an object-oriented programming language and a protocol-oriented programming language, and what the differences between the two programming paradigms are. In the example presented in this chapter, there were two major differences between the two designs.

The first major difference that we saw is that with protocol-oriented programming we should start with the protocol rather than a superclass. We can then use protocol extensions to add functionality to the types that conform to that protocol. With object-oriented programming, we started with a superclass. When we redesigned our example, we converted the `Vehicle` superclass to a `Vehicle` protocol, and then used a protocol extension to add the common functionality needed for all types that conform to the `Vehicle` protocol.

In the protocol-oriented example, we used protocol inheritance and protocol composition to allow us to create protocols with very specific requirements. This allowed us to create concrete types that only contained the functionality needed. In the object-oriented design, the concrete types inherited all of the functionality provided by the `Vehicle` superclass.

The second big difference that we saw was the use of value types (structures) rather than reference types (classes) for our vehicle types. Apple's documentation states that developers should prefer value types over reference types where appropriate. In our example, it was appropriate to use value types for the vehicle types. In Chapter 2, *Our Type Choices*, we will discuss the differences between value and reference types in depth.

Both the object-oriented design and the protocol-oriented design used polymorphism to let us interact with different types using a single interface. With the object-oriented design, we used the interface provided by the superclass to interact with all the subclasses. In the protocol-oriented design, we used the interface provided by the protocols and the protocol extensions to interact with the types that conform to the protocols.

Now that we have summarized the differences between object-oriented programming design and protocol-oriented programming design, let's take a closer look at these differences.

Differences between object-oriented programming and protocol-oriented programming

I mentioned at the beginning of the chapter that protocol-oriented programming is about so much more than just the protocol, and that it is a new way of not only writing applications, but also thinking about programming. In this section, we will examine the differences between our two designs to see what that statement really means.

As a developer, our primary goal is always to develop an application that works properly, but we should also be focused on writing clean and safe code. In this book, we will be talking about clean and safe code a lot, so let's look at what we mean by these terms.

Clean code is code that is very easy to read and understand. It is important to write clean code because any code that we write will need to be maintained by someone, and that someone is usually the person who wrote it. There is nothing worse than looking back at code you wrote and not being able to understand what it does. It is also a lot easier to find errors in code that is clean and easy to understand.

By safe code, we mean code that is hard to break. There is nothing more frustrating for us developers than making a small change in our code and then have errors pop up throughout the code base. By writing clean code, our code will be inherently safer because other developers will be able to look at the code and understand exactly what it does.

Now let's briefly look at the difference between protocols/protocol extensions and superclasses. We will be covering this a lot more in Chapter 4, *All About the Protocol*, and Chapter 5, *Let's Extend Some Types*.

Protocol and protocol extensions compared with superclasses

In the object-oriented programming example, we created a Vehicle superclass from which all of the vehicle classes were derived. In the protocol-oriented programming example, we used a combination of a protocol and a protocol extension to achieve the same result; however, there are several advantages in using protocols.

To refresh our memory of the two solutions, let's look at the code for both the Vehicle superclass and the Vehicle protocol and protocol extension. The following code shows the Vehicle superclass:

```
class Vehicle {
  fileprivate var vehicleTypes = [TerrainType]()
    fileprivate var vehicleAttackTypes = [TerrainType]()
    fileprivate var vehicleMovementTypes = [TerrainType]()
    fileprivate var landAttackRange = -1
    fileprivate var seaAttackRange = -1
    fileprivate var airAttackRange = -1
    fileprivate var hitPoints = 0

  func isVehicleType(type: TerrainType) -> Bool {
    return vehicleTypes.contains(type)
  }
  func canVehicleAttack(type: TerrainType) -> Bool {
    return vehicleAttackTypes.contains(type)
  }
  func canVehicleMove(type: TerrainType) -> Bool {
    return vehicleMovementTypes.contains(type)
  }
  func doLandAttack() {}
  func doLandMovement() {}
  func doSeaAttack() {}
  func doSeaMovement() {}
```

```
    func doAirAttack() {}
    func doAirMovement() {}
    func takeHit(amount: Int) { hitPoints -= amount }
    func hitPointsRemaining() -> Int { return hitPoints }
    func isAlive() -> Bool { return hitPoints > 0 ? true : false }
}
```

The `Vehicle` superclass is a complete type that we can create instances of. This can be a good or a bad thing. There are times, such as in this example, when we should not be creating instances of the superclass; we should only be creating instances of the subclasses. For this, we can still use protocols with object-oriented programming; however, we will need to use protocol extensions to add the common functionality, and that leads us down the protocol-oriented programming path.

Now let's look at how we used protocols and protocol extensions with protocol-oriented programming to create the `Vehicle` protocol and the `Vehicle` protocol extension:

```
protocol Vehicle {
    var hitPoints: Int {get set}
}
extension Vehicle {
    mutating func takeHit(amount: Int) { hitPoints -= amount }
    func hitPointsRemaining() -> Int { return hitPoints }
    func isAlive() -> Bool { return hitPoints > 0 ? true : false }
}
```

We then created three additional protocols, one for each type of vehicle, and used protocol inheritance to inherit the requirements and functionality from the `Vehicle` protocol into these three protocols. The following are the `LandVehicle`, `SeaVehicle`, and `AirVehicle` protocols:

```
protocol LandVehicle: Vehicle {
    var landAttack: Bool {get}
    var landMovement: Bool {get}
    var landAttackRange: Int {get}
    func doLandAttack()
    func doLandMovement()
}

protocol SeaVehicle: Vehicle {
    var seaAttack: Bool {get}
    var seaMovement: Bool {get}
    var seaAttackRange: Int {get}
    func doSeaAttack()
    func doSeaMovement()
}
```

```
protocol AirVehicle: Vehicle {
    var airAttack: Bool {get}
    var airMovement: Bool {get}
    var airAttackRange: Int {get}
    func doAirAttack()
    func doAirMovement()
}
```

The code in both of these solutions is pretty safe and easy to understand; however, the protocol-oriented design is safer. By separating the implementation from the definition and dividing the requirements into small, more specific protocols, we were able to eliminate the need for a bloated superclass, and also prevented types from inheriting functionality they do not need.

There are three clear advantages that protocols/protocol extensions have over superclasses. The first advantage is that types can conform to multiple protocols; however, they can only have one superclass. What this means is that we can create numerous protocols that contain very specific functionality rather than creating a single monolithic superclass. We can see this in our example where the `Vehicle` superclass contained the functionality for land, sea, and air vehicles; however while, in the protocol-oriented design, we were able to create three protocols, one for each type of vehicle.

The second advantage that protocol/protocol extensions have is that we can use protocol extensions to add functionality without needing the original code. What this means is that we can extend any protocol, even the protocols that are a part of the Swift language itself. To add functionality to our superclass, instead, we need to have the original code. We could use extensions to add functionality to a superclass, which means that all the subclasses will also inherit that functionality. However, generally, we use extensions to add functionality to a specific class rather than adding functionality to a class hierarchy.

The third advantage that protocols/protocol extensions have is that protocols can be adopted by classes, structures, and enumerations, while class hierarchies are restricted to class types. Protocols/protocol extensions give us the option to use value types where appropriate.

Implementing vehicle types

The implementations of vehicle types were slightly different between the object-oriented example and the protocol-oriented example however the difference is pretty significant. We will look at the differences between these two examples, but first, let's take a look at the code again to remind us how we implemented the vehicle types. We will look at how we implemented the Tank type in the object-oriented example first:

```
class Tank: Vehicle {
    override init() {
        super.init()
        vehicleTypes = [.Land]
        vehicleAttackTypes = [.Land]
        vehicleMovementTypes = [.Land]
        landAttackRange = 5

        hitPoints = 68
    }
    override func doLandAttack() { print("Tank Attack") }
    override func doLandMovement() { print("Tank Move") }
}
```

This class is a subclass of the Vehicle superclass, and it implements a single initializer. While this is a pretty simple and straightforward implementation, we really need to fully understand what the superclass expects in order to implement the type properly. For example, if we do not fully understand the Vehicle superclass, we may forget to set the landAttackRange property. In our example, forgetting to set this property will cause the instances of the Tank type unable to attack properly.

Now let's look at how we implemented a vehicle type in the protocol-oriented programming example:

```
struct Tank: LandVehicle {
    var hitPoints = 68
    let landAttackRange = 5
    let landAttack = true
    let landMovement = true
    func doLandAttack() { print("Tank Attack") }
    func doLandMovement() { print("Tank Move") }
}
```

The Tank type from the protocol-oriented design conforms to the LandVehicle protocol and uses the default initializer provided by the structure. The code in the protocol-oriented design is a lot safer and easier to understand. The reason we say that the protocol-oriented example is safer and easier to understand is because of the way properties and initializer are implemented in both the examples.

In the object-oriented programming example, all of the properties are defined in the superclass as variables. We will need to look at the code or the documentation for the superclass to see what properties are defined and how they are defined. If we forget to set something in a subclass, the compiler will happily compile the application and not warn us.

With protocols, we also need to look at the protocol itself or the documentation for the protocol to see which properties to implement. If we forget to implement any of the requirements, the compiler will warn us and refuse to compile until we properly set everything. We also have the ability to define any of the properties as constants, whereas with the object-oriented design we had to define them as variables.

The winner is...

As we were reading through this chapter, and seeing all of the advantages that protocol-oriented programming has over object-oriented programming, we may think that protocol-oriented programming is clearly superior to object-oriented programming. However, this assumption may not be totally correct.

Object-oriented programming has been around since the 1970s, and is a battle tested programming paradigm. Protocol-oriented programming is the new kid on the block, and was designed to correct some of the issues with object-oriented programming. I have personally used the protocol-oriented programming paradigm in a couple of projects and I am very excited about its possibilities.

Object-oriented programming and protocol-oriented programming have similar philosophies, such as creating custom types that can model real-world or virtual objects and polymorphism to use a single interface to interact with multiple types. The difference is in how these philosophies are implemented.

In my opinion, the code base in a project that uses protocol-oriented programming is much safer and easier to read as compared to a project that uses object-oriented programming. This does not mean that I am going to stop using object-oriented programming altogether; I can still see plenty of need for class hierarchy and inheritance.

Remember, when we are designing our application, we should always use the right tool for the right job. We would not want to use a chainsaw to cut a piece of 2 x 4 timber, but we also would not want to use a circular saw to cut down a tree. Therefore, the winner is the developer, where we have the choice of using different programming paradigms rather than being limited to only one.

Summary

In this chapter, we saw how Swift can be used as an object-oriented programming language and as a protocol-oriented programming language. While these two programming paradigms have similar philosophies, they implement these philosophies differently.

With object-oriented programming, we would use classes as our blueprints when we create objects. With protocol-oriented programming, we have the choice of using classes, structures, and enumerations. We can even use other types, as we will see in Chapter 2, *Our Type Choices*.

With object-oriented programming, we can implement polymorphism using class hierarchies. With protocol-oriented programming, we can use a combination of protocols and protocol extensions to implement polymorphism. We will look at protocols in depth in Chapter 4, *All About the Protocol*.

With object-oriented programming, we are able to implement functionality in our superclasses that is inherited by the subclasses. The subclasses do have the ability to override the functionality provided by their superclass. With protocol-oriented programming, we use protocol extensions to add functionality to types that conform to our protocols. These types can also shadow the protocol's default functionality if they choose to. We will look at protocol extensions in depth in Chapter 5, *Let's Extend Some Types*.

While object-oriented programming has been around since the 1970s it is beginning to show some wear and tear. In this chapter, we looked at the problems and design issues that protocol-oriented programming was designed to solve.

Now that we have seen an overview of protocol-oriented programming, it is time to look at the areas that make up protocol-oriented programming in greater detail. By achieving a deeper understanding of the different areas, we will be able to better implement protocol-oriented programming in our applications. We will start off by looking at the various type choices that we have with the Swift programming language and how we should use each of them.

2
Our Type Choices

In most traditional, object-oriented programming languages, we create classes (which are reference types) as blueprints for our objects. In Swift, unlike other object-oriented languages, structures have much of the same functionality as classes; however, they are value types. Apple has said that we should prefer value types, such as structures, to reference types, but what are the actual advantages? Swift actually has a number of type choices that we can use, and in this chapter we will look at each of these types to see the advantages and disadvantages of each. Knowing how and when to use each type is important in order to properly implement protocol-oriented programming in your projects.

In this chapter, you will learn the following:

- What a class is and how to use it
- What a structure is and how to use it
- What an enumeration is and how to use it
- What a tuple is and how to use it
- The difference between value and reference types

Swift classifies types as either named or compound types. A named type is a type that can be given a name when it is defined. These named types include classes, structures, enumerations, and protocols. In addition to user-defined named types, Swift also defines many commonly-used named types within the Swift standard library, including arrays, sets, and dictionaries.

Many of the data types that we would normally consider primitive types in other languages are actually named types in Swift and are implemented in the Swift standard library using structures. These include types that represent numbers, strings, characters, and Boolean values. Since these types are implemented as named types, we are able to extend their behavior using extensions as we would with any other named type. As we will see in both this and future chapters, the ability to extend a named type, including types that would traditionally be considered as primitive types and protocols, is an extremely powerful feature of the Swift language and is one of the pillars of protocol-oriented programming.

A compound type is a type that is not given a name when it is defined. In Swift, we have two compound types: Function types and tuple types. Function types represent closures, functions, and methods, while tuple types take the form of a comma-separated list that is enclosed in parentheses.

We are able to use the `typealias` declaration to give an alias to our compound types. This allows us to use the alias name instead of the type itself within our code.

There are two categories of types: Reference types and value types. When we pass an instance of a reference type, we are passing a reference to the original instance, which means that the two references are sharing the same instance. Classes are reference types. When we pass an instance of a value type, we are passing a new copy of the instance, which means that each instance is getting a unique copy. Value types include structures, enumerations, and tuples.

Every type in Swift will be either a named or compound type, and they will also be either a reference or value type, except in the case of protocols. Since we are unable to create an instance of a protocol, it is neither a reference nor a value type. Sound a bit confusing? It really isn't. As we look at all of our type choices and how we can use them, we will see how easy this is to understand.

Now, let's begin looking at the type choices that we have in Swift. We will begin by looking at the backbone of object-oriented programming: The class.

The class

In object-oriented programming, we cannot create an object without a blueprint that tells the application what properties and methods to expect from the object. In most object-oriented languages, this blueprint comes in the form of a class. A class is a construct that allows us to encapsulate the properties, methods, and initializers of an object into a single type. Classes can also include other items, such as subscripts; however, we are going to focus on the basic items that make up classes not only in Swift, but in other languages as well.

Let's look at how we would use a class in Swift. The following code shows how we defined the Tank class from Chapter 1, *Object-Oriented and Protocol-Oriented Programming*:

```
class Tank: Vehicle {
    override init() {
        super.init()
        vehicleTypes = [.Land]
        vehicleAttackTypes = [.Land]
        vehicleMovementTypes = [.Land]
        landAttackRange = 5

        hitPoints = 68
    }
    override func doLandAttack() { print("Tank Attack") }
    override func doLandMovement() { print("Tank Move") }
}
```

An instance of a class is typically called an object; however, in Swift, structures and classes have many of the same functionalities; therefore, we will use the term instance when referring to instances of either type.

Anyone who has used object-oriented programming in the past is probably familiar with the class type. It has been the backbone of object-oriented programming since its inception.

When we create instances of the class, it is named; therefore, the class is a named type. The class type is also a reference type.

The next type we are going to look at is arguably the most important type in the Swift language: The structure.

The structure

Apple said that Swift developers should prefer value types over reference types, and it seems that they have also taken that philosophy to heart. If we look at the Swift standard library (https://developer.apple.com/library/prerelease/ios/documentation/Gener al/Reference/SwiftStandardLibraryReference/index.html), we will see that the majority of the types are implemented using structures. The reason Apple is able to implement the majority of Swift's standard library with structures is that, in Swift, structures have many of the same functionalities as classes. There are, however, some fundamental differences between classes and structures, and we will be looking at these differences later in this chapter.

In Swift, a structure is a construct that allows us to encapsulate the properties, methods, and initializers of an instance into a single type. They can also include other items, such as subscripts. However, we are going to focus on the basic items that make up a structure. This description may sound a lot like how we described classes in the last section. This is because classes and structures are very similar in Swift. I know we have already mentioned this several times, but not only is it very important to understand the ways in which structures and classes are similar, but it is also necessary to understand the ways in which they are different in order to know which type to use.

Let's see how we could create a structure. The following example shows how we created the Tank structure in Chapter 1, *Object-Oriented and Protocol-Oriented Programming*, which has the same functionality as the Tank class:

```
struct Tank: LandVehicle {
    var hitPoints = 68
    let landAttackRange = 5
    let landAttack = true
    let landMovement = true
    func doLandAttack() { print("Tank Attack") }
    func doLandMovement() { print("Tank Move") }
}
```

If we compare this Tank structure to the Tank class from the previous section, we can see some very basic differences. In the Tank structure, we are not required to define an initializer because the structure will create a default initializer for us if we do not provide one to set the properties that need to be initialized. This default initializer will require us to provide initial values for all the properties that need values when we create an instance of the structure.

One difference that we do not see here is the `mutating` keyword used for some of the methods defined in the structures. Structures are value types; therefore, by default, the properties of the structure cannot be changed from within the instance methods. By using the `mutating` keyword, we are opting for the mutating behavior for that particular method. We must use the `mutating` keyword for any method within the structure that changes the values of the structure's properties.

The structure is a named type because, when we create instances of the type, it is named. The structure type is also a value type.

Let's look at how access controls work for classes and structures in Swift.

Access controls

There are times when we want to restrict access to certain parts of our code. This enables us to hide implementation details and only expose the interfaces we want to expose. This feature is handled by named access controls.

Access control allows us to restrict the access to, and visibility of, parts of our code. This allows us to hide implementation details and only expose the interfaces we want the external code to access. We can assign specific access levels to both classes and structures. We can also assign specific access levels to properties, methods, and initializers that belong to our classes and structures.

In Swift, there are four access levels:

- **Public**: This is the most visible access control level. It allows us to use the property, method, class, and so on anywhere we want to import the module. Basically, anything can use an item that has an access control level that is public. This level is primarily used by frameworks to expose the framework's public API.
- **Internal**: This is the default access level. This access level allows us to use the property, method, class, and so on in the defining source as well as the module that the source is in (the application or framework). If this level is used in a framework, it lets other parts of the framework use the item, but code outside the framework will be unable to access it.
- **Private**: This is the least visible access control level. It only allows us to use the property, method, class, and so on in the source file that defines it.
- **Fileprivate**: This access control was introduced in Swift 3. This access level restricts access to code defined in the same source file.

Access controls are extremely useful when we are developing frameworks. In order to use these frameworks, we would need to mark the public facing interfaces as public, so other modules, such as applications that import the framework, can use them. We would then use the internal and private access control levels to mark the interfaces that we want to use internally to the framework.

To define access levels, we place the name of the level before the definition of the entity. The following code shows examples of how we would add access levels to several entities:

```
private struct EmployeeStruct {}
public var firstName = "Jon"
internal var lastName = "Hoffman"
private var salaryYear = 0.0
public func getFullName() -> String {}
fileprivate func giveBonus(amount: Double) {}
```

There are some limitations with access controls, but these limitations are there to ensure that access levels in Swift follow a simple guiding principle—*no entity can be defined in terms of another entity that has a lower (more restrictive) access level*. What this means is that we cannot assign a higher (less restrictive) access level to an entity when it relies on another entity that has a lower (more restrictive) access level.

Here are a couple of examples to illustrate this rule:

- We cannot mark a method as being public when one of the arguments or the return type has an access level of private because external code would not have access to the private type
- We cannot set the access level of a method or property to public when the class or structure has an access level of private because external code would not be able to access the constructor when the class is private

The next type that we are going to look at is Swift's supercharged enumerations.

The enumerations

In most languages, enumerations are little more than a data type consisting of a set of named values called elements. In Swift, however, enumerations have been supercharged to give them significantly more power. Enumerations in Swift are a lot closer in functionality to classes and structures; however, they can still be used like enumerations in other languages.

Before we see how enumerations are supercharged in Swift, let's see how we can use them as standard enumerations. The following code defines an enumeration called `Devices`:

```
enum Devices {
   case IPod
   case IPhone
   case IPad
}
```

In the `Devices` enumeration, we defined three possible values: `IPod`, `IPhone`, and `IPad`.

One of the reasons why enumerations are different in Swift compared to other languages is that they can be prepopulated with values known as raw values. As shown in the following example, we could redefine our `Devices` enumeration to be prepopulated with `String` values:

```
enum Devices: String {
   case IPod = "iPod"
   case IPhone = "iPhone"
   case IPad = "iPad"
}
```

We can then use the `rawValue` property to retrieve the raw value for any of the enumeration's elements, as shown in the following code:

```
Devices.IPod.rawValue
```

In Swift, we can also store the associated values alongside our case values. These associated values can be of any type, and can vary for each case. This enables us to store additional custom information with our case types. Let's see how this works by redefining our `Devices` enumeration with the associated values:

```
enum Devices {
    case IPod(model: Int, year: Int, memory: Int)
    case IPhone(model: String, memory: Int)
    case IPad(model: String, memory: Int)
}
```

In the previous example, we defined three associated values with the `IPod` case and two associated values with the `IPhone` and `IPad` cases. We can then use this new `Devices` enumeration with the associated values, as follows:

```
var myPhone = Devices.IPhone(model: "6", memory: 64)
var myTablet = Devices.IPad(model: "Pro", memory: 128)
```

In this example, we defined the myPhone device as an iPhone 6 with 64 GB of memory and the myTablet device as iPod Pro with 128 GB of memory. We can now retrieve the associated values as follows:

```
switch myPhone {
case .IPod(let model, let year, let memory):
    print("iPod: (model) (memory)")
case .IPhone(let model, let memory):
    print("iPhone: (model) (memory)")
case .IPad(let model, let memory):
    print("iPad: (model) (memory)")
}
```

In this example, we will simply print out the associated values of the myPhone device.

What we have seen so far makes enumerations far more powerful than enumerations in other languages. However, we are not done showing off what enumerations can do in Swift. In Swift, enumerations are not limited to a list of elements. They can also contain computed properties, initializers, and methods, just like classes and structures.

Let's take a look at how we can use methods and computed properties with enumerations. Since it almost feels like Christmas with all of these exciting features, our example will have a holiday theme:

```
enum Reindeer: String {
    case Dasher, Dancer, Prancer, Vixen,
        Comet, Cupid, Donner, Blitzen, Rudolph
    static var allCases: [Reindeer] {
        return [Dasher, Dancer, Prancer, Vixen,
            Comet, Cupid, Donner, Blitzen, Rudolph]
    }
    static func randomCase() -> Reindeer {
        let randomValue = Int(
            arc4random_uniform(
                UInt32(allCases.count)
            )
        )
        return allCases[randomValue]
    }
}
```

In this example, we created an enumeration called Reindeer that contains the names of Santa's nine reindeer (we cannot forget Rudolph, you know). Within the Reindeer enumeration, we created an allCases computed property that returns an array containing all of the possible cases for the enumeration. We also created a randomCase() method that will return a random reindeer from our enumeration.

The previous examples in this section showed how to use the individual features of Swift's enumerations, but their true power is shown when they are used together. Let's take a look at one more example where we combine the associated values with methods and properties to make a supercharged enumeration. We will start off by defining a basic enumeration that defines the various formats of a book, with the page count and the price of each format stored in an associated value:

```
enum BookFormat {
    case PaperBack (pageCount: Int, price: Double)
    case HardCover (pageCount: Int, price: Double)
    case PDF (pageCount: Int, price: Double)
    case EPub (pageCount: Int, price: Double)
    case Kindle (pageCount: Int, price: Double)
}
```

This enumeration would work great, but there are some basic drawbacks. The first one, and the one that really drives me nuts, is seen when we retrieve the associated values from our enumerations. For example, let's create the following instance of the `BookFormat` enumeration:

```
var paperBack = BookFormat.PaperBack(pageCount: 220, price: 39.99)
```

Now, to retrieve the page count and the price of this enumeration, we could use the following code:

```
switch paperBack {
case .PaperBack(let pageCount, let price):
    print("(pageCount) - (price)")
case .HardCover(let pageCount, let price):
    print("(pageCount) - (price)")
case .PDF(let pageCount, let price):
    print("(pageCount) - (price)")
case .EPub(let pageCount, let price):
    print("(pageCount) - (price)")
case .Kindle(let pageCount, let price):
    print("(pageCount) - (price)")
}
```

This is quite a bit of code to retrieve the associated values, especially where we may need to retrieve these values in multiple locations throughout our code. We could create a global function that would retrieve these values, but we have a better way in Swift. We can add a computed property to our enumeration that will retrieve the pageCount and price values of the enumeration. The following example shows how we could add these computed properties:

```swift
enum BookFormat {
    case PaperBack (pageCount: Int, price: Double)
    case HardCover (pageCount: Int, price: Double)
    case PDF (pageCount: Int, price: Double)
    case EPub (pageCount: Int, price: Double)
    case Kindle (pageCount: Int, price: Double)
    var pageCount: Int {
        switch self {
        case .PaperBack(let pageCount, _):
            return pageCount
        case .HardCover(let pageCount, _):
            return pageCount
        case .PDF(let pageCount, _):
            return pageCount
        case .EPub(let pageCount, _):
            return pageCount
        case .Kindle(let pageCount, _):
            return pageCount
        }
    }
    var price: Double {
        switch self {
        case .PaperBack(_, let price):
            return price
        case .HardCover(_, let price):
            return price
        case .PDF(_, let price):
            return price
        case .EPub(_, let price):
            return price
        case .Kindle(_, let price):
            return price
        }
    }
}
```

With these computed properties, we can very easily retrieve the associated values from the `BookFormat` enumeration. The following code demonstrates how to use them:

```
var paperBack = BookFormat.PaperBack(pageCount: 220, price: 39.99)
print("(paperBack.pageCount) - (paperBack.price)")
```

These computed properties hide the complexity of the switch statement and provide a much cleaner dot syntax interface to use.

We can also add methods to our enumerations. Let's say, as an example, that if a person were to buy multiple copies of our book in different formats, they would receive a 20% discount. The following function could be added to our `BookFormat` enumeration to calculate this discount:

```
func purchaseTogether(otherFormat: BookFormat) -> Double {
    return (self.price + otherFormat.price) * 0.80
}
```

We could now use the method shown in the following code:

```
var paperBack = BookFormat.PaperBack(pageCount: 220, price: 39.99)
var pdf = BookFormat.PDF(pageCount: 180, price: 14.99)
var total = paperBack.purchaseTogether(otherFormat: pdf)
```

As we can see, enumerations in Swift are a lot more powerful than enumerations in most other languages. The one thing to avoid is overusing them. They are not meant to be a replacement for either the class or the structure. Deep down, enumerations are still a data type consisting of a finite set of named values, and all of these new exciting features are there to make them more useful to us.

When we create instances of the enumeration, it is named; therefore, it is a named type. The enumeration type is also a value type. Now let's look at one of the most underutilized types in Swift: The tuple type.

The tuple

In Swift, a tuple is a finite, ordered, comma-separated list of elements. While there are tuples in other languages that I have used, I never really took advantage of them. To be honest, I was only vaguely aware that they actually existed in those other languages. In Swift, tuples are more prominent than they are in other languages, which forced me to take a closer look at them. What I found is that they are extremely useful. In my opinion, tuples are one of the most underutilized types in Swift and, as we go through this book (especially in the case study section), I will point out some cases where the tuple type can be used.

We can create a tuple and access the information within it, as shown in the following example:

```
let mathGrade1 = ("Jon", 100)
let (name, score) = mathGrade1
print("(name) - (score)")
```

In the previous code, we grouped a `String` and an `Integer` into a single tuple type. We then decomposed the tuple using pattern matching, which places the values into the `name` and `score` constants.

What we saw in the last example is an unnamed tuple. These tuples work great in a pinch, but I have found that I use named tuples more often because it is much easier to retrieve the values from a named tuple. We can create a named tuple and access the information stored within it as shown in the following example:

```
let mathGrade2 = (name: "Jon", grade: 100)
print("(mathGrade2.name) - (mathGrade2.grade)")
```

Note that when we grouped the `String` and `Integer` values in this tuple, we assigned names to each of the values. We can then use these names to access the information within the tuple, thereby avoiding the decomposing step.

Apple has stated that we can use tuples as a return type for a function to return multiple values. The following example shows how we could use tuples to return multiple values from a function:

```
func calculateTip(billAmount: Double,tipPercent: Double) ->
    (tipAmount: Double, totalAmount: Double) {
        let tip = billAmount * (tipPercent/100)
        let total = billAmount + tip
        return (tipAmount: tip, totalAmount: total)
        }
```

In this example, we created a `calculateTip()` function that calculates the tip based on the `billAmount` and `tipPercentage` parameters that were passed in. We then returned both the tip amount that was calculated and also the total bill amount in a named tuple value.

We could then use this function as shown in the following code:

```
var tip = calculateTip(billAmount:31.98, tipPercent: 20)
print("(tip.tipAmount) - (tip.totalAmount)")
```

What we have seen in this section is how tuples are typically used in Swift. As we go through this book, we will be using tuples in various examples. Tuples are very useful when we need to pass a temporary collection of values in our code.

In Swift, a tuple is a value type. Tuples are also compound types; however, we are able to give a tuple an alias using the `typealias` keyword. The following example shows how we would assign an alias to a tuple:

```
typealias myTuple = (tipAmount: Double, totalAmount: Double)
```

In Swift, protocols are also considered a type.

Protocols

To some, it may seem surprising that protocols are considered a type since we cannot actually create an instance of them; however, we can use them as a type. What this statement means is that when we define the type for a variable, constant, tuple, or collection, we can use a protocol for that type.

We are not going to cover protocols in depth in this section since we have a whole chapter dedicated to them; however, it is important to understand that they are considered a type in Swift.

Each type that we have discussed so far is either a value or a reference type; however, a protocol is neither because we are not able to create an instance of them.

It is really important to have a complete understanding of the difference between value and reference types in Swift, so let's compare the two.

Value and reference types

There are some very fundamental differences between value types (structures, enumerations, and tuples) and reference types (classes). The primary difference is how the instances of value and reference types are passed. When we pass an instance of a value type, we are actually passing a copy of the original instance. This means that the changes made to one instance are not reflected back to the others. When we pass an instance of a reference type, we are passing a reference to the original instance. This means that both references point to the same instance; therefore, a change made to one reference will reflect in the others.

The explanation in the previous paragraph is a pretty straightforward explanation. We have seen this explanation a couple of times already in this book, but it is a very important concept that you must understand. In this section, we are going to examine the difference between value and reference types so that we know the advantages of each, as well as the pitfalls to avoid when using them.

Let's begin by creating two types. One is going to be a structure (value type) and the other is going to be a class (reference type). We will be using these types in this section to demonstrate the differences between value and reference types. The first type that we will look at will be named `MyValueType`. We will implement `MyValueType` using a structure, which means that it is a value type, as its name tells us:

```
struct MyValueType {
    var name: String
    var assignment: String
    var grade: Int
}
```

Within `MyValueType`, we defined three properties. Two of the properties are of the `String` type (name and assignment) and one is of the `Int` type (grade). Now, let's look at how we would implement this as a class:

```
class MyReferenceType {
    var name: String
    var assignment: String
    var grade: Int
    init(name: String, assignment: String, grade: Int) {
        self.name = name
        self.assignment = assignment
        self.grade = grade
    }
}
```

The `MyReferenceType` type defines the same three properties as the `MyValueType` type; however, we needed to define an initializer in the `MyReferenceType` type that we did not need to define in the `MyValueType` type. The reason for this is that structures provide us with a default initializer that will initialize all of the properties that need to be initialized if we do not provide a default initializer.

Let's look at how we could use each of these types. The following code shows how we could create instances of each of these types:

```
var ref = MyReferenceType(name: "Jon", assignment: "Math Test 1", grade:
90)
var val = MyValueType(name: "Jon", assignment: "Math Test 1", grade: 90)
```

As we see in this code, instances of structures are created in exactly the same way as the instances of classes. Being able to use the same format to create instances of structures and classes is good because it makes our lives easier. However, we need to keep in mind that value types behave in a different manner to reference types. Let's take a look at this. The first thing we need to do is create two functions that will change the grades for the instances of our two types:

```
func extraCreditReferenceType(ref: MyReferenceType, extraCredit: Int) {
    ref.grade += extraCredit
}

func extraCreditValueType(val: MyValueType, extraCredit: Int) {
    var val = val
    val.grade += extraCredit
}
```

Each of these functions takes an instance of one of our types and also an extra credit amount. Within the function, we will add the extra credit amount to the grade. Now let's see what happens when we use each of these functions. Let's start off by seeing what happens when we use the `MyReferenceType` type with the `extraCreditReferenceType()` function:

```
var ref =
MyReferenceType(name: "Jon", assignment: "Math Test 1", grade: 90)
extraCreditReferenceType(ref: ref, extraCredit:5)
print("Reference: (ref.name) - (ref.grade)")
```

In this code, we created an instance of the `MyReferenceType` type with a grade of 90. We then used the `extraCreditReferenceType()` function to add five extra points to the grade. If we run this code, the following line would be printed in the console:

Reference: Jon - 95

As we can see, five extra credit points were added to the grade. Now let's try to do the same thing with the `MyValueType` type and the `extraCreditValueType()` function. The following code shows how to do this:

```
var val =
MyValueType(name: "Jon", assignment: "Math Test 1", grade: 90)
extraCreditValueType(val: val, extraCredit:5)
print("Value: (val.name) - (val.grade)")
```

In this code, we created an instance of the `MyValueType` type with a grade of 90. We then used the `extraCreditValueType()` function to add five extra points to the grade. If we run this code, the following line would be printed in the console:

```
Value: Jon - 90
```

As we can see, the five extra credit points are missing from our grade in this example. The reason for this is when we pass an instance of a value type to a function, we are actually passing a copy of the original instance. This means that when we add the extra credit to the grade within the `extraCreditValueType()` function, we are adding it to a copy of the original instance. As a result, the changes are not reflected back to the original copy of the instance.

Using a value type protects us from making accidental changes to our instances because the instances are scoped to the function or type in which they are created. Value types also protect us from having multiple references to the same instance. Let's take a look at this so we can understand the type of issues we may face when we use reference types. We will begin by creating a function that is designed to retrieve the grade for an assignment from a data store. However, to simplify our example, we will simply generate a random score. The following code shows how we would write this function:

```
func getGradeForAssignment(assignment: MyReferenceType) {
    // Code to get grade from DB
    // Random code here to illustrate issue
    let num = Int(arc4random_uniform(20) + 80)
    assignment.grade = num
    print("Grade for (assignment.name) is (num)")
}
```

This function is designed to retrieve the grade for the assignment that is defined in the `MyReferenceType` instance that is passed into the function. Once the grade is retrieved, we will use it to set the `grade` property of the `MyReferenceType` instance. We will also print the grade out to the console so we can see what the grade is. Now, let's see how we would not want to use this function:

```
var mathGrades = [MyReferenceType]()
var students = ["Jon", "Kim", "Kailey", "Kara"]
var mathAssignment = MyReferenceType(name: "", assignment:
"Math Assignment", grade: 0)

for student in students {
    mathAssignment.name = student
    getGradeForAssignment(assignment: mathAssignment)
    mathGrades.append(mathAssignment)
}
```

In the previous code, we created a `mathGrades` array that will store the grades for our assignment and a `students` array that will contain the names of the students we wish to retrieve the grades for. We then created an instance of the `MyReferenceType` class that contains the name of our assignment. We will use this instance to request the grades from the `getGradeForAssignment()` function. Now that everything is defined, we will loop through the list of students to retrieve the grades. The following is a sample output from this code:

```
Grade for Jon is 90
Grade for Kim is 84
Grade for Kailey is 99
Grade for Kara is 89
```

This appears to look exactly like what we want. However, there is a huge bug in this code. Let's loop through our `mathGrades` array to see what grades we have in the array itself:

```
for assignment in mathGrades {
    print("(assignment.name): grade (assignment.grade)")
}
```

The output of this code would look as follows:

```
Kara: grade 89
Kara: grade 89
Kara: grade 89
Kara: grade 89
```

That is not what we wanted. The reason we see these results is because we created one instance of the `MyReferenceType` type and then we kept updating that single instance. This means that we kept overwriting the previous name and grade. Since `MyReferenceType` is a reference type, all the references in the `mathGrades` array pointed to the same instance of the `MyReferenceType` type, which ended up being Kara's grade.

Most veteran object-oriented developers have learned to watch out for this type of issue the hard way, but they occasionally still happen, especially with junior developers. Using value types can help us avoid these issues; however, there are times when we would like to have this type of behavior. Apple has provided a way for us to have this behavior with value types using the inout parameters. An inout parameter allows us to change the value of a value type parameter and to have that change persist after the function call has ended.

We define an inout parameter by placing the inout keyword at the start of the parameter's definition. An inout parameter has a value that is passed into the function. This value is then modified by the function and is passed back out of the function to replace the original value.

Let's look at how we can use value types with the inout keyword to create a version of the previous example that will work correctly. The first thing we need to do is modify the getGradesForAssignment() function to use an instance of MyValueType that it can modify:

```
func getGradeForAssignment(assignment: inout MyValueType) {
    // Code to get grade from DB
    // Random code here to illustrate issue
    let num = Int(arc4random_uniform(20) + 80)
    assignment.grade = num
    print("Grade for (assignment.name) is (num)")
}
```

The only change we made to this function was the way we defined the parameter that was passed in. The property is now defined as being of the MyValueType type, and we added the inout keyword to allow the function to modify the instance that was passed in. Now let's see how we could use this function:

```
var mathGrades = [MyValueType]()
var students = ["Jon", "Kim", "Kailey", "Kara"]
var mathAssignment = MyValueType(name: "", assignment: "Math Assignment",
grade: 0)

for student in students {
    mathAssignment.name = student
    getGradeForAssignment(assignment: &mathAssignment)
    mathGrades.append(mathAssignment)
}

for assignment in mathGrades {
    print("(assignment.name): grade (assignment.grade)")
}
```

Once again, this code looks a lot like the code from the previous example; however, we made two changes. The first is that the `mathAssignment` variable is now defined to be of the `MyValueType` type, and, when we called the `getGradeForAssignment()` function, we prefixed the argument with an ampersand (`&`). The ampersand tells us that we are passing a reference to the value type, so any changes made in the function are reflected back to the original instance.

The output of this new code will look as follows:

```
Grade for Jon is 97
Grade for Kim is 83
Grade for Kailey is 87
Grade for Kara is 85
Jon: grade 97
Kim: grade 83
Kailey: grade 87
Kara: grade 85
```

The output from this code is what we expected to see, where each instance in the `mathGrades` array represents a different grade. The reason this code works correctly is that when we add the `mathAssignment` instance to the `mathGrades` array, we are adding a copy of the `mathAssignment` instance to the array. However, when we pass the `mathAssignment` instance to the `getGradeForAssignment()` function, we are passing a reference, even though the type is a value type.

There are some things we cannot do with value types that we can do with reference (class) types. The first thing that we will look at is the recursive data type.

Recursive data types for reference types only

A recursive data type is a type that contains other values of the same type as a property for the type. Recursive data types are used when we want to define dynamic data structures, such as lists and trees. The size of these dynamic data structures can grow or shrink depending on our runtime requirements.

Linked lists are perfect examples of a dynamic data structure that we would implement using a recursive data type. A linked list is a group of nodes that are linked together, where, in its simplest form, each node maintains a link to the next node in the list. The following diagram shows how a very basic linked list works:

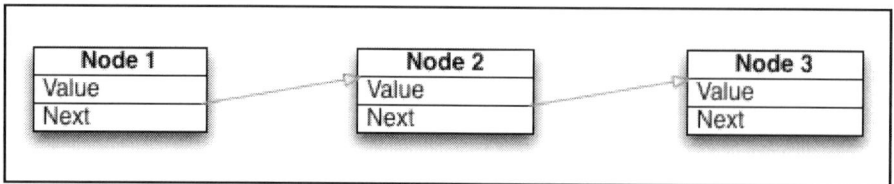

Each node in the list contains some value or data, and it also contains the link to the next node in the list. If one of the nodes within the list loses the reference to the next node, the remainder of the list will be lost because each node is only aware of the next node in the list. Some linked lists maintain a link to both the previous and next nodes to allow us to move both forward and backward through the list.

The following code shows how we could create a linked list using a reference type:

```
class LinkedListReferenceType {
    var value: String
    var next: LinkedListReferenceType?
    init(value: String) {
        self.value = value
    }
}
```

In the `LinkedListReferenceType` class, we have two properties. The first property is named `value` and contains the data for this instance. The second property is named `next`, which points to the next item in the linked list. If the `next` property is nil, then this instance would be the last node in the list. If we tried to implement this linked list as a value type, the code could look similar to the following code:

```
struct LinkedListValueType {
    var value: String
    var next: LinkedListValueType?
}
```

When we add this code to a playground, we receive the following error:

```
Recursive value type 'LinkedListValueType' is not allowed
```

This tells us that Swift does not allow recursive value types. However, we are able to implement them as a reference type, which we saw earlier.

If we think about it, recursive value types are a really bad idea because of how value types function. Let's examine this for a minute, because it will really stress the difference between value and reference types. It will also help you understand why we need reference types.

Let's say that we were able to create the `LinkedListValueType` structure without any errors. Now let's create three nodes for our list, as shown in the following code:

```
var one = LinkedListValueType(value: "One",next: nil)
var two = LinkedListValueType (value: "Two",next: nil)
var three = LinkedListValueType (value: "Three",next: nil)
```

Now we will link these nodes together with the following code:

```
one.next = two
two.next = three
```

Do you see the problem with this code? If not, think about how a value type is passed. In the first line, `one.next = two`, we are not actually setting the next property to the `two` instance itself; we are actually setting it to a copy of the `two` instance. This means that in the next line, `two.next = three`, we are setting the `next` property of the `two` instance itself to the `three` instance. However, this change is not reflected back in the copy that was made for the `next` property of the `one` instance. Sounds a little confusing? Let's clear it up a little by looking at a diagram that shows the state of our three `LinkedListValueType` instances if we were able to run this code:

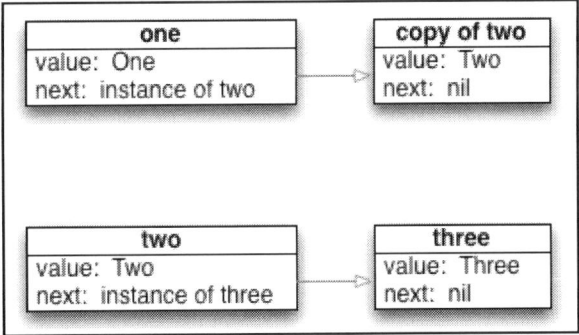

As we can see from the diagram, the `next` property of the `one` instance is pointing to a copy of the `two` instance whose `next` property is still nil. The `next` property of the original `two` instance, however, is pointing to the `three` instance. This means that if we try to go through the list by starting at the `one` instance, we would not reach the `three` instance because the copy of the `two` instance would still have a `next` property that is nil.

The second thing that we can only do with reference (class) types is class inheritance.

Inheritance for reference types only

In object-oriented programming, inheritance refers to one class (known as a sub or child class) being derived from another class (known as a super or parent class). The subclass will inherit methods, properties, and other characteristics from the superclass. With inheritance, we can also create a class hierarchy where we can have multiple layers of inheritance.

Let's look at how we could create a class hierarchy with the classes in Swift. We will start off by creating a base class named `Animal`:

```
class Animal {
    var numberOfLegs = 0
    func sleeps() {
        print("zzzzz")
    }
    func walking() {
        print("Walking on (numberOfLegs) legs")
    }
    func speaking() {
        print("No sound")
    }
}
```

In the `Animal` class, we defined one property (`numberOfLegs`) and three methods (`sleeps()`, `walking()`, and `speaking()`). Now, any class that is a subclass of the `Animal` class will also have these properties and methods. Let's see how this works by creating two classes that are subclasses of the `Animal` class. These two classes will be named `Biped` (an animal with two legs) and `Quadruped` (an animal with four legs):

```
class Biped: Animal {
    override init() {
        super.init()
        numberOfLegs = 2
    }
}

class Quadruped: Animal {
    override init() {
        super.init()
        numberOfLegs = 4
    }
}
```

Since these two classes inherit all of the properties and methods from the Animal class, all we need to do is create an initializer that sets the numberOfLegs property to the correct number of legs. Now, let's add another layer of inheritance by creating a Dog class that will be a subclass of the Quadruped class:

```
class Dog: Quadruped {
    override func speaking() {
        print("Barking")
    }
}
```

In the Dog class, we inherited from the Quadruped class that inherits from the Animal class. Therefore, the Dog class will have all of the properties, methods, and characteristics of both the Animal and Quadruped classes. If the Quadruped class overrides anything from the Animal class, then the Dog class will inherit the version from the Quadruped class.

We can create very complex class hierarchies in this manner. As an example, the following diagram expands on the class hierarchy that we just created to add several other animal classes:

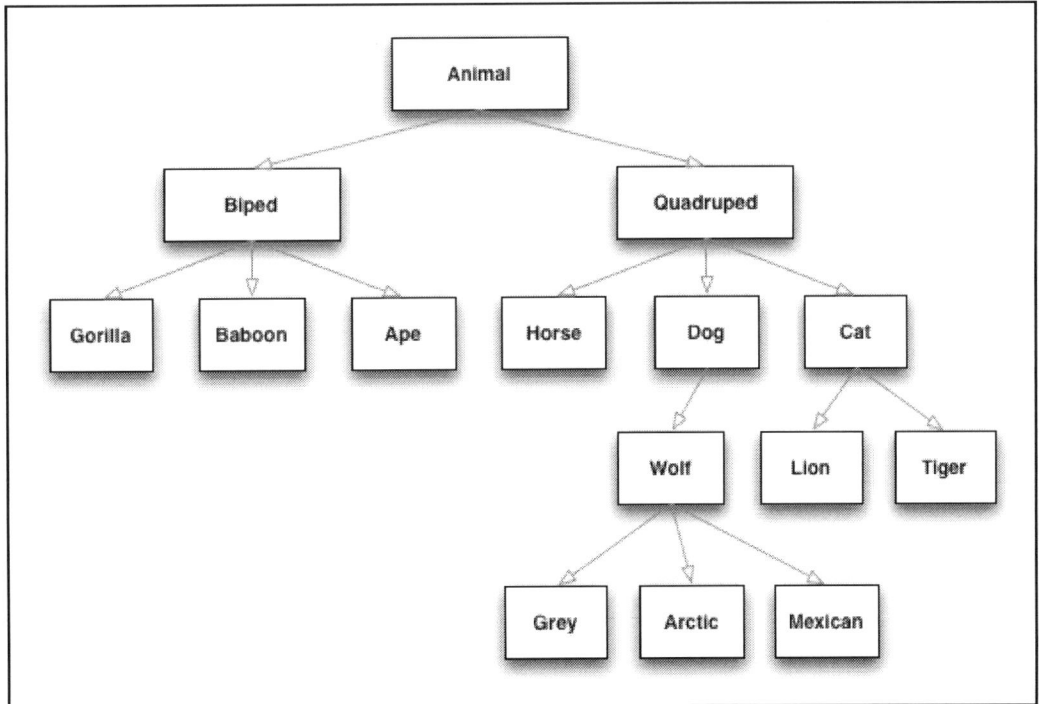

As we can see, class hierarchies can get very complex. However, as we just saw, they can eliminate a lot of duplicate code because our subclasses inherit methods, properties, and other characteristics from their superclasses. Therefore, we do not need to recreate them in all of the subclasses.

The biggest drawback of a class hierarchy is complexity. When we have a complex hierarchy, as shown in the preceding diagram, it is easy to make a change and not realize how it is going to affect all of the subclasses. As an example, if we think about the dog and cat classes, we may want to add a furColor property to our Quadruped class so we can set the color of the animal's fur. However, horses do not have fur; they have hair. So, before we can make any changes to a class in our hierarchy, we need to understand how it will affect all the subclasses in the hierarchy.

In Chapter 1, *Object-Oriented and Protocol-Oriented Programming*, we compared class hierarchies, such as the one here, to protocol-oriented programming. In Swift, it is best to avoid using complex class hierarchies, as shown in this example, and use a protocol-oriented approach, unless there are specific reasons to use them.

In most object-oriented languages, the standard library is in the form of a class hierarchy, where the majority of the library is implemented using classes, as shown in this section. However, Swift is a bit different.

Swift's built-in data types and data structures

If you are reading this book, you are probably very familiar with Swift's built-in data types and data structures. However, to really unleash their power, we need to understand how they are implemented in the Swift standard library.

The Swift standard library defines several standard data types, such as Int, Double, and String. In most languages, these types are implemented as primitive types, which means that they cannot be extended or subclassed. In Swift, however, these types are implemented in the Swift standard library as structures, which means we can extend these types just as we can with any other type that is implemented as a structure.

 You can read more about Swift's standard library at
https://developer.apple.com/library/prerelease/ios/documentation
/General/Reference/SwiftStandardLibraryReference/index.html.

Swift also defines several standard data structures, such as the array, dictionary, and set. Just like the built-in data types, these are also implemented as structures in the Swift standard library.

We will be discussing extensions in great detail in Chapter 5, *Let's Extend Some Types*, but right now, let's quickly see what we can do with extensions. As we will see, it is important to understand that data types and data structures in Swift are implemented with structures.

Let's say that, in our application, we needed to calculate the factorial of some integers. A factorial is written as 5!. To calculate a factorial, we take the product of all the positive integers less than or equal to the number. To calculate the factorial of 5, we will do as follows:

```
5! = 5*4*3*2*1
5! = 120
```

We could very easily create a global function to calculate the factorial, and we would do that in most languages. Extensions in Swift give us a better way to add functions such as this, and, since the Int type has been implemented as a structure, we can extend it, as shown in the following example:

```
extension Int {
    func factorial() -> Int {
    var answer = 1
    for x in (1...self).reversed() {
        answer *= x
        }
        return answer
    }
}
```

We could now calculate the factorial of any integer, as follows:

```
var f = 10
print(f.factorial())
```

It is sometimes better to extend a protocol rather than a single type, as shown here, because when we extend a protocol, all the types that conform to this protocol will receive the functionality rather than just the single type. We will discuss extensions in greater detail in Chapter 5, *Let's Extend Some Types*. The key point to keep in mind here is that any type derived from a named type can be extended, and most types in Swift that would normally be considered primitives in other languages are actually implemented with structures in Swift.

Summary

In most object-oriented programming languages, our type choices are pretty limited. In Swift, however, we have numerous choices. This allows us to use the right type for the right situation. The one type we did not cover too deeply is the protocol. That is because we will be covering protocols in more detail in Chapter 4, *All About the Protocol*. In this chapter, we also looked at the difference between value and reference types. This is a very important concept to understand, and we will be discussing it throughout this book.

3
Catching Our Errors

When I first started writing iOS and OS X applications with Objective-C, one of the most noticeable deficiencies was the lack of exception handling when working with the Cocoa and Cocoa Touch frameworks. Most modern programming languages (such as Java and C#) use `try-catch` blocks or something similar to handle exceptions. While Objective-C did have the `try-catch` block, it wasn't used within the Cocoa framework itself, and it never felt like a true part of the language. I have significant experience with C, so I was able to understand how the Cocoa and Cocoa Touch frameworks received and responded to errors; to be honest, I actually preferred this method, but I had grown accustomed to exception handling with Java and C#. When Swift was first introduced, I was hoping that Apple would put true error handling into the language so we would have the option of using it; however, it was not in the initial release. Finally, when Swift 2 was released, Apple did add additional error handling to Swift. While this error handling may look similar to exception handling in Java and C#, there are some very significant differences.

We will cover the following topics in this chapter:

- Using return values to handle errors
- Using Swift 2 error handling
- How to use the `guard` statement
- How to use the `defer` keyword
- When to use each of the error handling patterns

Error handling is the process of responding to, and recovering from, error conditions within our applications. Prior to Swift 2.0, error handling followed the same patterns that we used in Objective-C. Swift 2.0 introduced additional options. In this chapter, we will be covering the various options for error handling so we can see the advantages and disadvantages of the different options.

When we design our applications or frameworks, it is important that we properly respond to and recover from errors. This can be the difference between a successful or a failed launch of our applications. With proper error handling, our applications can respond to improper input or less than ideal conditions (network connection drops or data files becoming corrupt) and inform the user what went wrong. Without proper error handling, our applications could crash, causing user frustration and bad reviews. Error handling may not be one of the first things that you think of when you think about protocol-oriented programming, but it should be one of the first things you think about when you are designing your applications and frameworks.

In the simplest form of error handling, the return value from the function will indicate whether the function was successful or not. This return value could be something as simple as a Boolean true/false value, or something more complex, such as an enumeration or a tuple, whose values indicate what actually went wrong if the function was unsuccessful.

Swift 2.0 introduced a new way to handle errors. Languages such as Java and C# generally refer to the error handling process as exception handling; within the Swift documentation, Apple refers to this process as error handling. While, on the outside, Java and C# exception handling may look very similar to Swift's error handling, there are some significant differences.

In this chapter, we will be looking at different ways to handle errors in Swift and examine when and how we should use each. We will begin by looking at the guard statement, as we will be using this statement in the examples for this chapter.

Using the guard statement

In Swift and most modern languages, our conditional statements tend to focus on testing for true conditions. As an example, the following code tests to see whether the x variable is greater than 10. If so, we perform some function; otherwise, we handle the error condition:

```
var x = 9
if x > 10 {
  //Business Logic
} else {
  // Do error condition
}
```

This type of code leads us to having our business logic code embedded within conditional statements and the error conditions tucked away at the end. While we may be used to reading code such as this, because that is how we handle errors in most modern languages, it does make our code a challenge to read at times, especially if we need to do several checks. Wouldn't it be nice if we could handle error conditions at the beginning of our code and get them out of the way? I know in our simple example we could easily check if x is less than or equal to 10, and if so perform the error condition, but not all conditional statements are that easy to rewrite, especially items such as optional binding. Soon, we will look at how we would write a function that uses optional binding at the beginning of the code to check for nil values, but first let's define a structure named Blog, which we will use to demonstrate the guard statement. This structure will contain three optional properties:

```
struct Blog {
    var author: String?
    var name: String?
    var url: NSURL?
}
```

Now let's write a function that takes one parameter of the optional type that could contain either nil or an instance of the Blog type. Within the function, we will print out information about the blog; however, we will need to make sure that the parameter is not nil and also that the author and name properties are not nil. Here is the code for that function:

```
func blogInfo(blog: Blog?) {
    if let blog = blog {
        if let author = blog.author, let name = blog.name{
            print("BLOG:")
            print(" Author: \(author)")
            print(" name: \(name)")
        } else {
            print("Author or name is nil")
        }
    } else {
        print("Blog is nil")
    }
}
```

In the blogInfo(blog:) function, we have two optional binding statements to check if the blog parameters are nil and also if the author or name properties are nil. We could combine these into one optional binding statement. However, in this example we want separate messages for each check; therefore, we will use two separate optional binding statements.

As we can see in this example, our functional code is embedded within the two optional binding statements and our error messages are at the end of the function. If we want to see how we are handling each error condition, we need to follow the brackets for the `if` statements. If the function has 50 to 60 lines of functional code it can be hard to trace. Luckily, our IDEs can fold our code to make it a little easier to read, but it would be even easier to use the `guard` statement.

The `guard` statement is designed to transfer program control out of the current scope if a condition is not met. This allows us to trap errors and perform the error checks early in our functions/methods/initializers. This makes our code much easier to read and understand. Keep in mind that, whenever we make our code easier to read and understand, we make it safer, less error-prone, and easier to maintain. We could rewrite our previous example using the `guard` statement in this way:

```
func blogInfo2(blog: Blog?) {
    guard let blog = blog else {
        print("Blog is nil")
        return
    }
    guard let author = blog.author, let name = blog.name else {
        print("Author or name is nil")
        return
    }
    print("BLOG:")"
    print(" Author: \(author)")
    print(" name: \(name)")
}
```

In this example, we created a function named `blogInfo2(blog:)` that accepts an optional parameter named `blog` containing either an instance of the `Blog` type or a `nil` value. We then used two `guard` statements with optional binding. The first `guard` statement is used to verify that the `blog` parameter is not `nil`. The second `guard` statement is used to verify that the `author` and `name` properties do not contain `nil` values. If they do contain `nil` values, then the code within the `guard` statements is executed. Notice that each `guard` statement contains a `return` statement. This is because `guard` statements must contain a transfer of control statement, such as the `return` statement.

What is really nice about using the `guard` statement with optional binding is that the new variable that is created is in scope for the rest of the function, rather than just within the scope of the optional binding statement. This means we are able to use the `blog`, `author`, and `name` variables throughout the `blogInfo2(blog:)` function.

As we can see, it is much easier to read and understand the code within the
`blogPost2(blog:)` function that uses the `guard` statements compared with the
`blogInfo(blog:)` function, which uses `if-else` statements to perform the same
functionality.

Error handling

Now let's explore how we can do error handling in Swift. To demonstrate the two error
handling methods, we will use the `Drink` structure as shown in the following code:

```
struct Drink {
    var volume: Double
    var caffeine: Double
    var temperature: Double
    var description: String
    mutating func drinking(amount: Double) {
        volume -= amount
    }
    mutating func temperatureChange(change: Double) {
        temperature += change
    }
}
```

For each error handling pattern, we will add a single error condition for the `drinking()`
method that is returned or thrown if the `amount` parameter (which specifies how much we
are drinking) is greater than the `volume` property (which defines the amount remaining in
the drink). We will also define two error conditions for the `temperatureChange()` method
that will be returned or thrown if the drink gets too hot or too cold.

Now let's begin with our error handling patterns. The first pattern that we will show is how
to use return values to indicate success or failure.

Error handling with return values

Error handling, in its simplest form, uses the return value from a function or method to
indicate whether it was successful or not. This return value could be something as simple as
a Boolean true/false value or something more complex, such as an enumeration, whose
values indicate what actually went wrong if the function or method was unsuccessful.

Let's see how we would use the return value to add error handling to the `drinking()` method of the `Drink` structure. For this function, we just need an indicator that will let us know if we were able to successfully take the drink or not. This is the ideal situation for using a Boolean return value. A return value of `true` will indicate that the function was successful, and a return value of `false` will indicate that it failed. Let's see how we would implement this with the `drinking()` method:

```
mutating func drinking(amount: Double) -> Bool {
    guard amount <= volume else {
        return false
    }
    volume -= amount
    return true
}
```

In this method, we use the `guard` statement to verify that the amount that we want to drink is less than or equal to the volume remaining in the drink. If not, we return a `false` value indicating that the method failed; otherwise, we subtract the amount we drank from the volume remaining in the drink and return a `true` value, indicating that the method was successful.

Adding a simple Boolean return value to our methods is one of the easiest ways to add error handling to our applications. It is also very easy to check for errors with this type of error handling. For example, the following code creates an instance of the `Drink` class and then uses the `drinking()` method to take a drink. We then verify that we successfully took a drink:

```
var myDrink = Drink(volume: 23.5, caffeine: 280,
    temperature: 38.2,
    description: "Drink Structure")

if myDrink.drinking(amount: 50.0) {
    print("Had a drink")
} else {
    print("Error")
}
```

In this code, to check for errors, all we need to do is call to the `drinking()` method in an `if` statement to verify that the method was successful.

Now let's look at how we would use a return value to indicate whether the temperature of the drink is still in the acceptable range after a call to the `temperatureChange()` method. The return value for the method will be an enumeration that will let us know if the temperature of the drink is too cold, too hot, or just right. This enumeration will look like this:

```
enum DrinkTemperature {
    case TooHot
    case TooCold
    case JustRight
}
```

Now let's see how we would change the `temperatureChange()` method to let us know whether the temperature of the drink is within the acceptable range:

```
mutating func temperatureChange(change: Double) -> DrinkTemperature {
    temperature += change
    guard temperature >= 35 else {
        return .TooCold
    }
    guard temperature <= 45 else {
        return .TooHot
    }
    return .JustRight
}
```

The acceptable range of temperature for our drinks is between 35 and 45 degrees; therefore, in our code we need to verify that the temperature of the drink is greater than or equal to 35 degrees and less than or equal to 45 degrees. In our new method, we use a `guard` statement to verify that the drink is greater than or equal to 35 degrees; otherwise, we return a `TooCold` value. We then use another `guard` statement to verify that the drink is less than or equal to 45 degrees; otherwise, we return a `TooHot` value. If the temperature successfully passes the two `guard` statements, we return a `JustRight` value.

We would use this function like this:

```
var results = myDrink.temperatureChange(change: -5)
switch results {
case .TooHot:
    print("Drink too hot")
case .TooCold:
    print("Drink too cold")
case .JustRight:
    print("Drink just right")
}
```

In this example, we used a `switch` statement after we changed the temperature to see if the temperature of the drink got too hot, too cold, or was still in the acceptable range. We could use an `if` statement if all we wanted to do was verify that the temperature was in an acceptable range.

If we needed additional information about our error, we could use associated values with the enumeration. In this example, the additional information could be the actual temperature of the drink.

What we saw in this section is the easiest error handling pattern to implement; however, there are several drawbacks to this pattern. The biggest drawback to this error handling pattern is that it is very easy to ignore the errors. This can cause issues in our application if we simply assume a function/method was successful when it isn't.

As a general rule, if a function/method has a return value we should always check it to verify that the function completed successfully.

Error handling with do-catch

On the surface, exception handling in languages such as Java and C# may look very similar to Swift's error handling pattern; however, there are some significant differences. Developers accustomed to exception handling with these languages will notice these differences as they read this section. Before we explore how this error handling works, we need to see how to represent errors.

Representing errors

In Swift, errors are represented by values of types that conform to the `Error` protocol. Swift's enumerations are very well suited for modeling these error conditions because, generally, we have a finite number of error conditions to represent. We can also use associated values to add additional information about the errors.

Let's look at how we could use an enumeration to represent an error. For this, we will define a fictitious error named `MyError` with three error conditions: `Minor`, `Bad`, and `Terrible`:

```
enum MyError: Error {
    case Minor
    case Bad
    case Terrible
}
```

In this example, we define that the `MyError` enumeration conforms to the `Error` protocol. We then define the three error conditions: `Minor`, `Bad`, and `Terrible`. We can also use the associated values with our error conditions to give additional information about the error that occurred. If we wanted to add a description to one of the error conditions, we would do it like this:

```
enum MyError: Error {
    case Minor
    case Bad
    case Terrible (description: String)
}
```

Those who are familiar with exception handling in Java and C# can see that representing errors in Swift is a lot cleaner and easier. Another advantage that we have is that it is very easy to define multiple error conditions and group them together so that all the related error conditions are of one type.

Let's see how we would represent the error conditions for the `Drink` type:

```
enum DrinkErrors: Error {
    case insufficentVolume
    case tooHot
    case tooCold
}
```

We begin by defining that the `DrinkErrors` enumeration conforms to the `Error` protocol. Within the `DrinkErrors` enumeration, we define our three error conditions that could occur within the `Drink` structure. As we mentioned earlier in this section, we can use associated values with our `Error` enumerations. With associated values, we could rewrite our `DrinkErrors` enumeration like this:

```
enum DrinkErrors: Error {
    case insufficentVolume
    case tempOutOfRange (Description: String)
}
```

This is a perfectly acceptable way to define errors in Swift; however, it is not recommended to define them in this way. When an error is thrown in an application, we want to make sure we can catch the specific error so we know how to react to it. In this example, we would be able to catch the `tempOutOfRange` error as it was thrown, but we would then need to do an additional lookup to find out whether the temperature was too high or too low. Having to do this additional lookup would not be ideal and would add additional complexity that is not necessary.

If we are going to use associated values with our error types, the associated values should be used to add additional information about the error condition rather than being used to specify the type of error that occurred. For example, we could use associated values to return the actual temperature, as shown in the following example:

```
enum DrinkErrors: Error {
    case insufficentVolume
    case tooHot (temp: Double)
    case tooCold (temp: Double)
}
```

Now that we have seen how to define errors, let's look at how we would throw an error if an error condition occurred.

Throwing errors

When an error occurs in a function, the code that called the function must be made aware of it; this is called **throwing the error**. When a function throws an error, it assumes that the code that called it, or some code further up the chain, will catch and recover appropriately from the error.

To throw an error from a function or method, we use the `throws` keyword. This keyword lets the code that called it know that an error may be thrown. Unlike exception handling in other languages, we do not list the specific error types that may be thrown.

 Since we do not list the specific error types that may be thrown from a function within the function's definition, it would be good practice to list them in the documentation and comments for the function so that other developers who use our function know what error types to catch.

Let's look at how we would throw errors in Swift. We will start by seeing how we would throw an error for our `drinking()` method. This method will throw an error if we do not have enough volume left in our drink. The error that is thrown will be the `insufficentVolume` **error:**

```
/// This method will take a drink from our drink if we have
/// enough liquid left in our drink.
/// - parameter amount: The amount to drink
/// - throws: DrinkError.insufficientVolume if there is not
/// enough volume left
  mutating func drinking(amount: Double) throws {
      guard amount < volume else {
          throw DrinkErrors.insufficientVolume
      }
```

```
        volume -= amount
    }
```

Note how we start the `drinking()` method with a comment. This comment block starts off by describing what the method does. We then describe what the `amount` parameter is, and, finally, we list the errors that could be thrown by this method. When we use comments as shown in this example, we are able to hold down the *option* key and then click on the function name anywhere in our code. Xcode will then display a popup with the description of the function, as shown in the following screenshot:

If you are using Swift for Linux or any other operating system, I would still recommend commenting your code with this method for consistency purposes.

Using comments in the way we have just demonstrated will help us document what our method does, what type of parameters it accepts, the return value, and what type of errors are thrown from the method. Earlier we mentioned that we do not specify the types of errors thrown from our functions, methods, or initializers, but if we document our code as shown here, we can document the error types that could be thrown and what the errors mean.

When we define the `drinking()` method, we define it with the `throws` keyword at the end of the declaration. The `throws` keyword indicates that a function, method, or initializer can throw an error. If our function or method had a return type, the `throws` keyword will appear after the parameter list but before the return type. The following example shows how we would use the `throws` keyword if we had a return value:

```
func myFunc(parm: String) throws -> String
```

Within the `drinking()` method, we use the `guard` statement to verify that we have enough volume left to take our drink. If we do not have enough volume left in the drink, we throw the `DrinkErrors.insufficentVolume` error. To throw an error, we use the `throw` keyword followed by the error we wish to throw. When an error is thrown, control is returned to the code that called the function or method.

Now let's look at how we would write the `temperatureChange()` method that could throw either the `DrinkErrors.tooHot` or `DrinkErrors.tooCold` error:

```
/// This method will change the temperature of the drink.
/// - parameter change: The amount to change, can be negative
///     or positive
///
/// - throws:
///     - DrinkError.tooHot if the drink is too hot
///     - DrinkError.tooCold if the drink is too cold
mutating func temperatureChange(change: Double) throws {
    temperature += change
    guard temperature > 35 else {
        throw DrinkErrors.tooCold(temp: temperature)
    }
    guard temperature < 45 else {
        throw DrinkErrors.tooHot(temp: temperature)
    }
}
```

In the `temperatureChange()` method, we use comments in much the same way as we use them in the `drinking()` method to document what the method does and also what errors could be thrown. Within the method itself, we begin by adjusting the temperature of the drink. We then use two `guard` statements that verify whether the temperature of the drink is still within the acceptable range. If the temperature is outside the acceptable range, we throw either the `DrinkErrors.tooHot` or `DrinkErrors.tooCold` error.

Now let's look at how we would catch the errors that are thrown.

Catching errors

When an error is thrown from a function, we need to catch it in our code; this is done using the `do-catch` block. The `do-catch` block takes the following syntax:

```
do {
    try [Some function that throws an error]
} catch [pattern] {
    [Code if function threw error]
}
```

When we call a function or method that throws an error, we must prefix the call with the `try` keyword. The `try` keyword helps us quickly identify the code that could potentially throw errors.

If an error is thrown, it is propagated out until it is handled by a `catch` clause. The `catch` clause consists of the `catch` keyword, followed by a pattern to match the error against. If the error matches the pattern, the code within the `catch` block is executed.

Let's see how we would catch the errors thrown from the `drinking()` method:

```
do {
    try myDrink.drinking(amount: 50.0)
} catch DrinkErrors.insufficentVolume {
    print("Error taking drink")
}
```

In this example, we surrounded the call to the `drinking()` method with the `do-catch` block, and we also prefixed the call to the `drinking()` method with the `try` keyword. The catch statement attempts to match the `DrinkErrors.insufficentVolume` error since that is the error thrown by the `drinking()` method.

If the `DrinkErrors.insufficentVolume` error is thrown from the `drinking()` method, we then print the message `Error taking drink` to the console.

We do not have to include a pattern after the `catch` statement. If a pattern is not included after the `catch` statement, or we put an underscore, the `catch` statement will match all error conditions. For example, either one of the following two `catch` statements will catch all errors:

```
do {
    // our statements
} catch {
    // our error conditions
}

do {
    // our statements
} catch _ {
    // our error conditions
}
```

If we are unsure of the errors that may be thrown from a function or method, it is a good idea to include a `catch` statement that will match all error conditions to avoid having an error at runtime that is not caught. If we have an error at runtime that is not caught, the application will crash.

If we want to capture the error, we can use the `let` keyword, as shown in the following example:

```
do {
    // our statements
} catch let error {
    print("Error: \(error)")
}
```

Now let's see how we would catch the `DrinkErrors.tooHot` and `DrinkErrors.tooCold` errors from the `temperatureChange()` method:

```
do {
    try myDrink.temperatureChange(change: 20.0)
} catch DrinkErrors.tooHot(let temp) {
    print("Drink too hot: \(temp) degrees ")
} catch DrinkErrors.tooCold(let temp) {
    print("Drink too cold: \(temp) degrees ")
}
```

In this example, we have two `catch` statements where each `catch` statement matches a different error condition. In addition, we also capture the associated value for the error by using the `let` statement within the parentheses, as shown in this example.

When I am working with exceptions in languages such as Java and C#, I see a lot of empty `catch` blocks. This is where we need to catch the exceptions because one might be thrown; however, we do not want to do anything with it. In Swift, the code would look something like this:

```
do {
    try myDrink.temperatureChange(change: 20.0)
} catch {}
```

Seeing code like this is one of the things that I dislike about exception handling. The Swift developers have an answer for this: the `try?` keyword. The `try?` keyword attempts to perform an operation that may throw an error. If the operation succeeds, the results, if any, are returned in the form of an optional; however, if the operation fails, with an error being thrown, the operation returns a `nil` and the error is discarded. We would use the `try?` keyword like this:

```
try? myDrink.temperatureChange(20.0)
```

If the function or method had a return type, we would use optional binding to capture the value returned, as shown in the next example:

```
if let value = try? myMethod(42) {
        print("Value returned \(value)")
}
```

As we can see, the `try?` keyword makes our code much cleaner and easier to read.

We can also let the errors propagate out rather than immediately catching them. To do this, we just need to add the `throws` keyword to the function definition. For instance, in the following example, rather than catching the error, we let it propagate out to the code that called the function:

```
func myFunc() throws {
    try myDrink.temperatureChange(20.0)
}
```

If we need to perform some clean up action, regardless of whether we had any errors or not, we can use the `defer` statement.

Using the defer statement

We use the defer statement to execute a block of code just before the code execution leaves the current scope. The following example shows how we would use the defer statement:

```
func deferFunction()  {
    print("Function started")
    var str: String?
    defer {
        print("In defer block")
        if let s = str {
            print("str is \(s)")
        }
    }
    str = "Jon"
    print("Function finished")
}
```

If we called this function, the first line that is printed to the console is Function started. The execution of the code skips the defer block, and Function finished would then be printed to the console. Finally, the defer code block will be executed just before we leave the function's scope, and we see the message In defer block. The following is the output from this function:

```
Function started
Function finished
In defer block
str is Jon
```

The defer block will always be called before the execution leaves the current scope, even if an error is thrown. The defer block is very useful when we need to perform some clean up functions prior to leaving a function.

The defer statement is very useful when we want to make sure we perform all the necessary clean up, even if an error is thrown. For example, if we successfully open up a file to write to, we will always want to make sure we close that file, even if we have an error during the write operation. We could then put the file-closed functionality in a defer block to make sure that the file is always closed prior to leaving the current scope.

In this chapter, we saw two ways that we can do error handling in Swift, but which one should we use?

When to use error handling

There were two distinct error handling patterns that we saw in this chapter:

- Error handling with return values
- Error handling with `do-catch` blocks

Now that we have explored these two error handling patterns, we need to decide when to use each one. In order to help us understand which error handling pattern to use, we need to really understand the advantages and disadvantages of each.

Error handling with return values is definitely the easiest error handling pattern to implement. In this pattern, the value that is returned from a method or function indicates whether we had an error or not. This return value could be something as simple as a Boolean `true` value (indicating success) or a `false` value (indicating failure). The return value could also be something more complex, such as an enumeration whose values would indicate specific success or failure conditions.

Error handling with the `do-catch` block is the error handling pattern that was first introduced with Swift 2. This pattern is very easy to use, but it does add additional complexity that is sometimes not needed when we simply want to know if a function was successful or not.

Let's think about how we would use each of these error handling patterns. Let's say that we have a function that checks to see what type of network connection we have. Our return values may be an enumeration that could contain the following values: `WIFI`, `MOBILE`, or `NONETWORK`. In this function, if an error occurs while checking the network connection, we would generally want to set the network type to `NONETWORK` and have our code assume that there is no network connection. This would be a great candidate for handling errors with return values.

In this scenario, if we need additional information about the errors that occurred, we could add additional enumeration values. We could also throw the error using the `do-catch` block; however, that may be overkill if our code simply treats any error with the network check as not having a network connection.

Now let's assume that we have a function that retrieves values from a data source (a web service or database). Simply returning a nil value to indicate that our data source is not available may not be enough, because we would also return a nil value if no value was found. In this scenario, we should use Swift's error handling pattern. This will allow us to return a nil value if the value was not found, or throw an error to let the code know that the data source is not available. Our code would probably want to treat these two conditions separately.

Summary

Error handling is the process of responding to, and recovering from, error conditions within our applications. In this chapter, we looked at two different error handling patterns that we can use in Swift. Knowing when to use each (and using it appropriately) can make our applications and frameworks safer and easier to maintain.

In the next chapter, we will look at how and why we should use protocols.

4
All About the Protocol

Coming from an object-oriented background, I am very familiar with protocols (or interfaces, as they are known in other object-oriented languages). However, prior to Apple introducing protocol-oriented programming, protocols, or interfaces, were rarely the focal point of my application designs, unless I was working with an **Open Service Gateway Initiative (OSGi)**-based project. When I designed an application in an object-oriented way, I always began the design with the objects. The protocols or interfaces were then used where they were appropriate, mainly for polymorphism when a class hierarchy did not make sense. Now, all that has changed, and with protocol-oriented programming, the protocol has been elevated to the focal point of our application design.

In this chapter you will learn the following:

- How to define property and method requirements within a protocol
- How to use protocol inheritance and composition
- How to use a protocol as a type
- What polymorphism is
- How to use associated values with a protocol
- How to use the delegation pattern in Swift
- How to design type requirements with protocols

When we are designing an application in an object-oriented way, we begin the design by focusing on the objects and how they interact. The object is a data structure that contains information about the attributes of the object in the form of properties, and the actions performed by or to the object in the form of methods. We cannot create an object without a blueprint that tells the application what attributes and actions to expect from the object. In most object-oriented languages, this blueprint comes in the form of a class. A class is a construct that allows us to encapsulate the properties and actions of an object into a single type.

Most object-oriented programming languages contain an interface type. This interface is a type that contains method and property signatures, but does not contain any implementation details. An interface can be considered a contract where any type that conforms to the interface must implement the required functionality defined within it.

Interfaces in most object-oriented languages are primarily used as a way to achieve polymorphism. There are some frameworks, such as OSGi, that use interfaces extensively; however, in most object-oriented designs, the interface takes a back seat to the class and class hierarchy.

Designing an application in a protocol-oriented way is significantly different from designing it in an object-oriented way. As we stated earlier, object-oriented design begins with the objects and the interaction between the objects, while protocol-oriented design begins with the protocol. While protocol-oriented design is about so much more than just the protocol, we can think of the protocol as the backbone of protocol-oriented programming. After all, it would be pretty hard to have protocol-oriented programming without the protocol.

A protocol in Swift is similar to interfaces in object-oriented languages, where the protocol acts as a contract that defines the methods, properties, and other requirements needed by our types to perform their tasks. We say that the protocol acts as a contract because any type that adopts, or conforms, to the protocol promises to implement the requirements defined by the protocol.

Any class, structure, or enumeration can conform to a protocol. A type cannot conform to a protocol unless it implements all required functionality defined within the protocol. If a type adopts a protocol and it does not implement all functionality defined by the protocol, we will get a compile time error and the project will not compile.

Most modern object-oriented programming languages implement their standard library with a class hierarchy; however, the basis of Swift's standard library is the protocol (https ://developer.apple.com/library/prerelease/ios/documentation/General/Referenc e/SwiftStandardLibraryReference/index.html). Therefore, not only does Apple recommend that we use the protocol-oriented programming paradigm in our applications, but they also use it in the Swift standard library.

With the protocol being the basis of the Swift standard library and also the backbone of the protocol-oriented programming paradigm, it is very important that we fully understand what the protocol is and how we can use it. In this chapter, we will go over the basic usage of the protocol, which will include the syntax for defining the protocol, how to define requirements in a protocol, and how to make our types conform to a given protocol. At the end of this chapter, we will look at how to implement the delegation pattern in Swift using protocols and how to use protocol composition to create small, very specific protocols rather than large monolithic ones.

Protocol syntax

In this section, we will look at how to define a protocol, define requirements within a protocol, and specify that a type conforms to a protocol.

Defining a protocol

The syntax we use to define a protocol is very similar to the syntax used to define a class, structure, or enumeration. The following example shows the syntax used to define a protocol:

```
protocol MyProtocol {
  //protocol definition here
}
```

To define the protocol, we use the `protocol` keyword followed by the name of the protocol. We then put the requirements, which our protocol defines, between curly brackets. Custom types can state that they conform to a particular protocol by placing the name of the protocol after the type's name, separated by a colon. The following example shows how we would state that the `MyStruct` structure conforms to the `MyProtocol` protocol:

```
struct MyStruct: MyProtocol {
  //structure implementation here
}
```

A type can also conform to multiple protocols. We list the multiple protocols that the type conforms to by separating them with commas. The following example shows how we would specify that the `MyStruct` structure type conforms to the `MyProtocol`, `AnotherProtocol`, and `ThirdProtocol` protocols:

```
struct MyStruct: MyProtocol, AnotherProtocol, ThirdProtocol {
  // Structure implementation here
}
```

Having a type conform to multiple protocols is a very important concept within protocol-oriented programming, as we will see later in the chapter. This concept is known as protocol composition.

Now let's see how we would add property requirements to our protocol.

Property requirements

A protocol can require that the conforming types provide certain properties with specified names and types. The protocol does not say whether the property should be a stored or computed property because the implementation details are left up to the conforming types.

When defining a property within a protocol, we must specify whether the property is a read-only or a read-write property by using the `get` and `set` keywords. We also need to specify the property's type since we cannot use the type inference in a protocol. Let's look at how we would define properties within a protocol by creating a protocol named `FullName`, as shown in the next example:

```
protocol FullName {
  var firstName: String {get set}
  var lastName: String {get set}
}
```

In the `FullName` protocol, we define two properties named `firstName` and `lastName`. Both of these properties are defined as read-write properties. Any type that conforms to the `FullName` protocol must implement these properties. If we wanted to define the property as read-only, we would define it using only the `get` keyword, as shown in the following code:

```
var readOnly: String {get}
```

It is possible to define static properties by using the `static` keyword as shown in the following example:

```
static var typeProperty: String {get}
```

Now let's see how we would add method requirements to our protocol.

Method requirements

A protocol can require that the conforming types provide specific methods. These methods are defined within the protocol exactly as we define them within a class or structure, but without the curly brackets and method body. We can define that these methods are instance or type methods using the `static` keyword. Adding default values to the method's parameters is not allowed when defining the method within a protocol.

Let's add a method named `getFullName()` to our `FullName` protocol:

```
protocol FullName {
    var firstName: String {get set}
    var lastName: String {get set}

    func getFullName() -> String
}
```

Our `fullName` protocol now requires one method named `getFullName()` and two read-write properties named `firstName` and `lastName`.

For value types, such as the structure, if we intend for a method to modify the instances that it belongs to, we must prefix the method definition with the `mutating` keyword. This keyword indicates that the method is allowed to modify the instance it belongs to. The following example shows how to use the `mutating` keyword with a method definition:

```
mutating func changeName()
```

If we mark a method requirement as mutating, we do not need to write the `mutating` keyword for that method when we adopt the protocol with a reference (class) type. The mutating keyword is only used with value (structures or enumerations) types.

Optional requirements

There are times when we want protocols to define optional requirements—that is, methods or properties that are not required to be implemented. To use optional requirements, we need to start off by marking the protocol with the `@objc` attribute.

 It is important to note that only classes can adopt protocols that use the `@objc` attribute. Structures and enumerations cannot adopt these protocols.

To mark a property or method as optional, we use the `optional` keyword. Let's look at how we would use the `optional` keyword to define optional properties and methods:

```
@objc protocol Phone {
  var phoneNumber: String {get set}
  @objc optional var emailAddress: String {get set}
  func dialNumber()
  @objc optional func getEmail()
}
```

In the `Phone` protocol we just created, we define a required property named `phoneNumber` and an optional property named `emailAddress`. We also defined a required function named `dialNumber()` and an optional function named `getEmail()`.

Now let's explore how protocol inheritance works.

Protocol inheritance

Protocols can inherit requirements from one or more additional protocols and then add additional requirements. The following code shows the syntax for protocol inheritance:

```
protocol ProtocolThree: ProtocolOne, ProtocolTwo {
    // Add requirements here
}
```

The syntax for protocol inheritance is very similar to class inheritance in Swift, except that we are able to inherit from more than one protocol. Let's see how protocol inheritance works. We will use the `FullName` protocol that we defined earlier in this section and create a new protocol named `Person`:

```
protocol Person: FullName {
    var age: Int {get set}
}
```

Now, when we create a type that conforms to the `Person` protocol, we must implement the requirements defined in the `Person` protocol, as well as the requirements defined in the `FullName` protocol. As an example, we could define a `Student` structure that conforms to the `Person` protocol as shown in the following code:

```
struct Student: Person {
    var firstName = ""
    var lastName = ""
    var age = 0
    func getFullName() -> String {
        return "(firstName) (lastName)"
    }
}
```

Note that in the `Student` structure, we implemented the requirements defined in both the `FullName` and `Person` protocols; however, the only protocol specified when we defined the `Student` structure was the `Person` protocol. We only needed to list the `Person` protocol because it inherited all of the requirements from the `FullName` protocol.

Now let's look at a very important concept in the protocol-oriented programming paradigm: protocol composition.

Protocol composition

Protocol composition lets our types adopt multiple protocols. This is a major advantage that we get when we use protocols rather than a class hierarchy because classes, in Swift and other single-inheritance languages, can only inherit from one superclass. The syntax for protocol composition is the same as the protocol inheritance that we just saw. The following example shows how to do protocol composition:

```
struct MyStruct: ProtocolOne, ProtocolTwo, Protocolthree {
    // implementation here
}
```

Protocol composition allows us to break our requirements into many smaller components rather than inheriting all requirements from a single superclass or class hierarchy. This allows our type families to grow in width rather than height, which means we avoid creating bloated types that contain requirements that are not needed. Protocol composition may seem like a very simple concept, but it is a concept that is essential to protocol-oriented programming. Let's look at an example of protocol composition so we can see the advantage we get from using it.

Let's say that we have the class hierarchy shown in the following diagram:

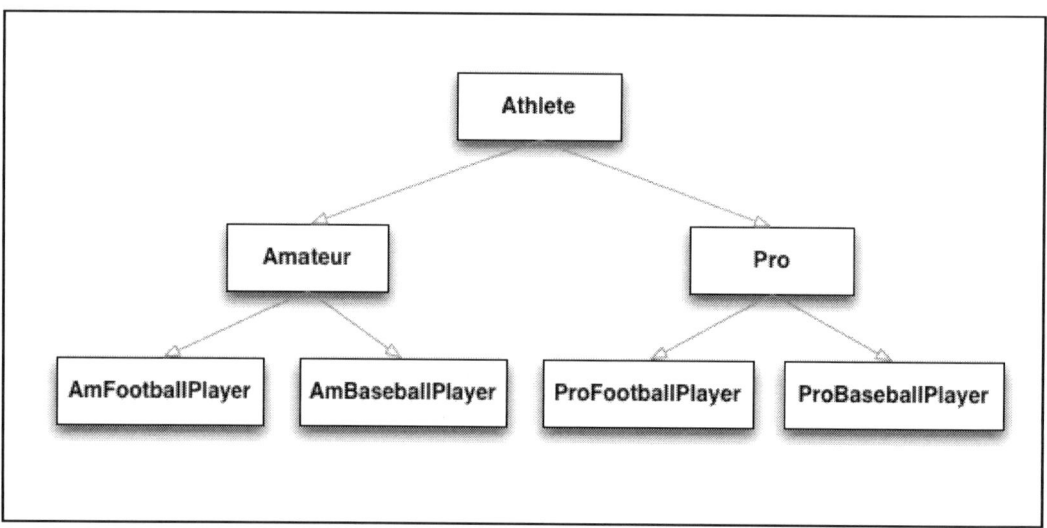

In this class hierarchy, we have a base class named `Athlete`. The `Athlete` base class then has two subclasses named `Amateur` and `Pro`. These classes are used depending on whether the athlete is an amateur athlete or a pro athlete. An amateur athlete may be a collegiate athlete, and we would need to store information such as which school they go to and their GPA. A pro athlete is one that gets paid for playing the game. For the pro athletes, we would need to store information such as what team they play for and their salary.

In this example, things get a little messy under the `Amateur` and `Pro` classes. As we can see, we have a separate football player class under both the `Amateur` and `Pro` classes (the `AmFootballPlayer` and `ProFootballPlayer` classes). We also have a separate baseball class under both the `Amateur` and `Pro` classes (the `AmBaseballPlayer` and `ProBaseballPlayer` classes). This will require us to have a lot of duplicate code between these classes.

With protocol composition, instead of having a class hierarchy where our subclasses inherit all functionality from a single superclass, we have a collection of protocols that we can mix and match in our types.

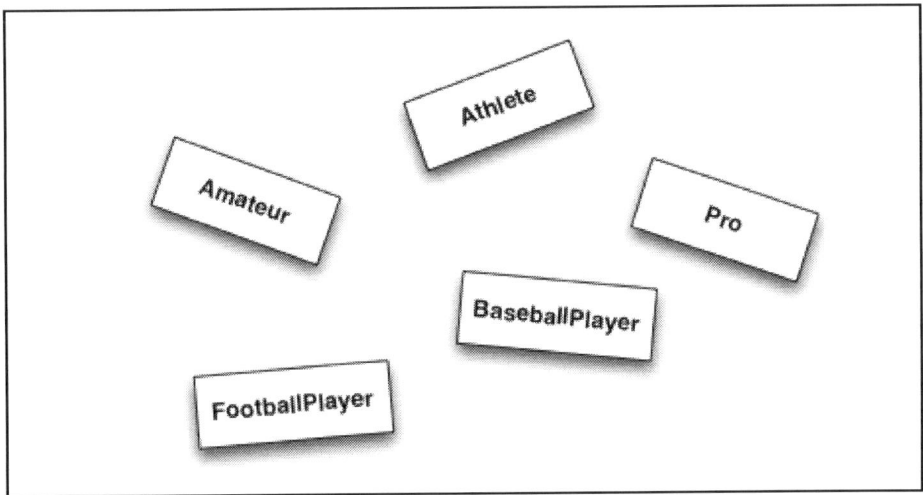

We then use one or more of these protocols as needed for our types. For example, we can create an `AmFootballPlayer` structure that conforms to the `Athlete`, `Amateur`, and `FootballPlayer` protocols. We could also create the `ProFootballPlayer` structure that conforms to the `Athlete`, `Pro`, and `FootballPlayer` protocols. This allows us to be very specific about the requirements for our types and only adopt the requirements that we need.

From a pure protocol point of view, this last example may not make a lot of sense right now because protocols only define the requirements. In `Chapter 5`, *Let's Extend Some Types*, we will look at this example again to see how protocol extensions can be used to implement these types with minimal duplicate code.

 One word of warning: If you find yourself creating numerous protocols that only contain one or two requirements in them, then you are probably making your protocols too granular. This will lead to a design that is hard to maintain and manage.

Now let's look at how a protocol is a full-fledged type in Swift.

Using protocols as a type

Even though no functionality is implemented in a protocol, they are still considered a full-fledged type in the Swift programming language, and can mostly be used like any other type. What this means is that we can use protocols as parameters or return types for a function. We can also use them as the type for variables, constants, and collections. Let's take a look at some examples. For these next few examples, we will use the following PersonProtocol protocol:

```
protocol PersonProtocol {
    var firstName: String {get set}
    var lastName: String {get set}
    var birthDate: Date {get set}
    var profession: String {get}
    init (firstName: String, lastName: String, birthDate: Date)
}
```

In this PersonProtocol, we define four properties and one initializer.

For this first example, we will show how to use a protocol as a parameter and return type for a function, method, or initializer. Within the function itself, we also use the PersonProtocol as the type for a variable:

```
func updatePerson(person: PersonProtocol) -> PersonProtocol {
var newPerson: PersonProtocol
// Code to update person goes here
  return newPerson
  }
```

We can also use protocols as the type to store in a collection, as shown in the next example:

```
var personArray = [PersonProtocol]()
var personDict = [String: PersonProtocol]()
```

The one thing we cannot do with protocols is to create an instance of one. This is because no functionality is implemented within a protocol. As an example, if we tried to create an instance of the PersonProtocol protocol, as shown in the following example, we would receive the error; error: protocol type 'PersonProtocol' cannot be instantiated:

```
var test = PersonProtocol(firstName: "Jon", lastName: "Hoffman", birthDate:
birthDateProgrammer)
```

We can use the instance of any type that conforms to our protocol anywhere that the protocol type is required. As an example, if we define a variable to be of the PersonProtocol protocol type, we can then populate that variable with the instance of any type that conforms to the PersonProtocol protocol. Let's assume that we have two types named SwiftProgrammer and FootballPlayer that conform to the PersonProtocol protocol. We can then use them as shown in this next example:

```
var myPerson: PersonProtocol

myPerson = SwiftProgrammer(firstName: "Jon", lastName: "Hoffman",
birthDate: birthDateProgrammer)

myPerson = FootballPlayer(firstName: "Dan", lastName: "Marino", birthDate:
birthDatePlayer)
```

In this example, the myPerson variable is defined to be of the PersonProtocol protocol type. We can then set this variable to instances of either of the SwiftProgrammer and FootballPlayer types. One thing to note is that Swift does not care if the instance is a class, structure, or enumeration. It only matters that the type conforms to the PersonProtocol protocol type.

As we saw earlier, we can use our PersonProtocol protocol as the type for an array, which means that we can populate the array with instances of any type that conforms to the PersonProtocol protocol. The following is an example of this (note that the bDateProgrammer and bDatePlayer variables are instances of the Date type that would represent the birth date of the individual):

```
var programmer = SwiftProgrammer(firstName: "Jon", lastName: "Hoffman",
birthDate: bDateProgrammer)

var player = FootballPlayer(firstName: "Dan", lastName: "Marino",
birthDate: bDatePlayer)

var people: [PersonProtocol] = []
people.append(programmer)
people.append(player)
```

What we are seeing in these last couple of examples is a form of polymorphism. To use protocols to their fullest potential, we need to understand what polymorphism is.

Polymorphism with protocols

The word polymorphism comes from the Greek roots *poly* (meaning many) and *morphe* (meaning form). In programming languages, polymorphism is a single interface to multiple types (many forms). There are two reasons to learn the meaning of the word polymorphism. The first reason is that using such a fancy word can make you sound very intelligent in casual conversation. The second reason is that polymorphism provides one of the most useful programming techniques not only in object-oriented programming, but also protocol-oriented programming.

Polymorphism lets us interact with multiple types through a single uniform interface. In the object-oriented programming world the single uniform interface usually comes from a superclass, while in the protocol-oriented programming world, that single interface usually comes from a protocol.

In the last section, we saw two examples of polymorphism with Swift. The first example was the following code:

```
var myPerson: PersonProtocol

myPerson = SwiftProgrammer(firstName: "Jon", lastName: "Hoffman",
birthDate: bDateProgrammer)

myPerson = FootballPlayer(firstName: "Dan", lastName: "Marino", birthDate:
bDatePlayer)
```

In this example, we had a single variable of the `PersonProtocol` type. Polymorphism allowed us to set the variable to instances of any type that conforms to the `PersonProtocol` protocol, such as the `SwiftProgrammer` or `FootballPlayer` types.

The other example of polymorphism was in the following code:

```
var programmer = SwiftProgrammer(firstName: "Jon", lastName: "Hoffman",
birthDate: bDateProgrammer)

var player = FootballPlayer(firstName: "Dan", lastName: "Marino",
birthDate: bDatePlayer)

var people: [PersonProtocol] = []
people.append(programmer)
people.append(player)
```

In this example, we created an array of `PersonProtocol` types. Polymorphism allowed us to add instances of any types that conform to `PersonProtocol` to this array.

When we access an instance of a type through a single uniform interface, as we just showed, we are unable to access type-specific functionality. As an example, if we had a property in the `FootballPlayer` type that records the age of the player, we would be unable to access that property because it is not defined in the `PeopleProtocol` protocol.

If we do need to access type-specific functionality, we can use type casting.

Type casting with protocols

Type casting is a way to check the type of an instance and/or to treat the instance as a specified type. In Swift, we use the `is` keyword to check whether an instance is of a specific type and the `as` keyword to treat an instance as a specific type.

The following example shows how we would use the `is` keyword:

```
if person is SwiftProgrammer {
    print("(person.firstName) is a Swift Programmer")
}
```

In this example, the conditional statement returns `true` if the `person` instance is of the `SwiftProgrammer` type or `false` if it isn't. We can also use the `switch` statement (as shown in the next example) if we want to check for multiple types:

```
for person in people {
    switch (person) {
    case is SwiftProgrammer:
        print("(person.firstName) is a Swift Programmer")
    case is FootballPlayer:
        print("(person.firstName) is a Football Player")
    default:
        print("(person.firstName) is an unknown type")
    }
}
```

We can use the `where` statement in combination with the `is` keyword to filter an array to only return instances of a specific type. In the next example, we filter an array that contains instances of the `PersonProtocol` to only return those elements of the array that are instances of the `SwiftProgrammer` type:

```
for person in people where person is SwiftProgrammer {
    print("(person.firstName) is a Swift Programmer")
}
```

Now let's look at how we would cast an instance to a specific type. To do this, we can use the `as` keyword. Since the cast can fail if the instance is not of the specified type, the `as` keyword comes in two forms: `as?` and `as!`. With the `as?` form, if the casting fails it returns a nil; with the `as!` form, if the casting fails we get a runtime error. Therefore, it is recommended to use the `as?` form unless we are absolutely sure of the instance type or we perform a check of the instance type prior to doing the cast.

The following example shows how we would use the `as?` keyword to attempt to cast an instance of a variable to the `SwiftProgammer` type:

```
if let _ = person as? SwiftProgrammer {
    print("(person.firstName) is a Swift Programmer")
}
```

Since the `as?` keyword returns an optional, in the last example we could use optional binding to perform the cast. If we are sure of the instance type, we can use the `as!` keyword as shown in the next example:

```
for person in people where person is SwiftProgrammer {
  let p = person as! SwiftProgrammer
}
```

Now let's see how we can use associated types with protocols.

Associated types with protocols

When defining a protocol, there are times when it is useful to define one or more associated types. An associated type gives us a placeholder name that we can use within the protocol in place of a type. The actual type to use for the associated type is not defined until the protocol is adopted. The associated type basically says; *we do not know the exact type to use; therefore, when a type adopts this protocol it will define it*. As an example, if we were to define a protocol for a queue, we would want the type that adopts the protocol to define the instance types that the queue contains rather than the protocol.

To define an associated type, we use the `associatedtype` keyword. Let's see how to use associated types within a protocol. In this example, we will define the QueueProtocol protocol that will define the requirements needed to implement a queue:

```
protocol QueueProtocol {
    associatedtype QueueType
    mutating func addItem(item: QueueType)
    mutating func getItem() -> QueueType?
    func count() -> Int
}
```

In this protocol, we define one associated type named QueueType. We then use this associated type twice within the protocol. We use it first as the parameter type for the addItem() method. We then use it again when we define the return type of the getItem() method as an optional type that might return an instance defined by the QueueType associated type; of course, it might also return nil.

Any type that implements the QueueProtocol protocol must specify the type to use for the QueueType placeholder, and must also ensure that only items of that type are used where the protocol uses the QueueType placeholder.

Let's look at how to implement QueueProtocol in a non-generic class called IntQueue. This class will implement the QueueProtocol protocol using the Int type:

```
struct IntQueue: QueueProtocol {
  var items = [Int]()
  mutating func addItem(item: Int) {
    items.append(item)
  }
  mutating func getItem() -> Int? {
    if items.count > 0 {
      return items.remove(at: 0)
    }
    else {
      return nil
    }
  }
  func count() -> Int {
    return items.count
  }
}
```

As we can see in the `IntQueue` structure, we use the `Int` type for both the parameter type of the `addItem()` method and the return type of the `getItem()` method. These are the same types that were defined as the `QueueType` associated type in the `QueueProtocol` protocol.

In the preceding example, we implemented the `QueueProtocol` protocol in a non-generic way. Generics in Swift allow us to define the type to use at runtime rather than compile time. We cover generics more in `Chapter 6`, *Working with Generics*. Let's see how to implement the `QueueProtocol` protocol as a generic type called `GenericQueue`:

```
class GenericQueue<T>: QueueProtocol {
    var items = [T]()
    func addItem(item: T) {
        items.append(item)
    }
    func getItem() -> T? {
        if items.count > 0 {
            return items.remove(at: 0)
        } else {
            return nil
        }
    }
    func count() -> Int {
        return items.count
    }
}
```

The `GenericQueue` implementation is very similar to the `IntQueue` implementation, except that we define the type to use with the generic placeholder `T`. We can then use the `GenericQueue` class as we would use any generic type. Let's take a look at how to use the `GenericQueue` class:

```
var intQ2 = GenericQueue<Int>()
intQ2.addItem(2)
intQ2.addItem(4)
print(intQ2.getItem())
intQ2.addItem(6)
```

Now that we have explored protocols in some detail, let's look at how we would implement the delegation design pattern using protocols.

Delegation

Delegation is used extensively within the Cocoa and Cocoa Touch frameworks. The delegation pattern is a very simple but powerful pattern where an instance of one type acts on behalf of another instance. The instance that is doing the delegating keeps a reference to the delegate instance, and then, when an action happens, the delegating instance sends a message to the delegate, who performs the intended function. Sounds confusing? It really isn't.

This design pattern is implemented in Swift by creating a protocol that defines the delegates' responsibilities. The type that conforms to the protocol, known as the delegate, will adopt this protocol, guaranteeing that it will provide the functionality defined by the protocol.

Let's look at an example of the delegation pattern in Swift. For this example, we will have a `Person` structure. This structure will have two properties of the `String` type, named `firstName` and `lastName`. It will also have a third property that will store the delegate instance. When either the `firstName` or `lastName` properties are set, we will call a method in the delegate instance that will display the full name. Since the `Person` structure is delegating the responsibility for displaying the name to another instance, it does not need to know or care how the name is being displayed. Therefore, the full name could be displayed in a console window or in a `UILabel`; alternatively, the message may be ignored altogether.

Let's start off by looking at the protocol that defines the delegate's responsibilities. We will name this delegate `DisplayNameDelegate`:

```
import Foundation

protocol DisplayNameDelegate {
    func displayName(name: String)
}
```

In the `DisplayNameDelegate` protocol, we define one method that the delegate needs to implement named `displayName()`. It is assumed that within this method the delegate will somehow display the name; however, it is not required. The only requirement is that the delegate implements this method.

Now let's look at the `Person` structure. This is the structure that will do the delegation:

```
import Foundation

struct Person {
    var displayNameDelegate: DisplayNameDelegate
```

```
      var firstName = "" {
          didSet {
              displayNameDelegate.displayName(name: getFullName())
          }
      }
      var lastName = "" {
          didSet {
              displayNameDelegate.displayName(name: getFullName())
          }
      }

      init(displayNameDelegate: DisplayNameDelegate) {
          self.displayNameDelegate = displayNameDelegate
      }

      func getFullName() -> String {
          return "(firstName) (lastName)"
      }
  }
```

In the `Person` structure, we start off by adding our three properties, which are named `displayNameDelegate`, `firstName`, and `lastName`. The `displayNameDelegate` property contains an instance of our delegate type. This instance will be responsible for displaying the full name when the values of the `firstName` and `lastName` properties change.

Within the definitions for the `firstName` and `lastName` properties, we define the property observers. The property observers are called each time the value of the properties is changed. Within these property observers, we call the `displayName()` method of our delegate instance, which is responsible for displaying the name.

Now let's create a type that will conform to the `DisplayNameDelegate` protocol. We will name this type `MyDisplayNameDelegate` and implement the `displayName()` method defined in the protocol:

```
  struct MyDisplayNameDelegate: DisplayNameDelegate {
      func displayName(name: String) {
          print("Name: (name)")
      }
  }
```

In this example, all we do is print the name to the console. Now let's see how we would use this delegate:

```
var displayDelegate = MyDisplayNameDelegate()
var person = Person(displayNameDelegate: displayDelegate)

person.firstName = "Jon"
person.lastName = "Hoffman"
```

In this code, we begin by creating an instance of the `MyDisplayNameDelegate` type and then use that instance to create an instance of the `Person` type. We then assign the name of `Jon` to the `firstName` property. When the value of the `firstName` property changes, the property observer that we set is called, which calls the delegate to display the name; as a result, the value of `Jon` is printed to the console. Finally, we set the `lastName` property to `Hoffman`. Just like the `firstName` property, when the value of the `lastName` property changes, the property observer that we set is called, which then calls the delegate to display the name. This time the value `Jon Hoffman` is printed to the console.

Displaying values to the console like this really does not show off the power of the delegation pattern. Within the downloadable code for this book there is a simple project named `Delegation` that shows how we can use the delegation pattern to display the name within a `UILabel` whenever the values of the names change.

If you download the code for the delegation project, you will notice that the `DisplayNameDelegate` protocol and the `Person` structure are exactly the same as the example in the book. This is one of the many advantages of using the delegation pattern. Since the type that is delegating the functionality does not care how the delegate implements the functionality (in our example, it displays the name to the console), we can reuse the code within a single project or across multiple projects.

Another advantage that we get from using the delegation pattern is loose coupling. In our example, we separated the logic part of our code from the view by using the delegate to display the name whenever the `firstName` or `lastName` properties changed. Loose coupling promotes a separation of responsibility, where each type is responsible for very specific tasks; this makes it very easy to swap out these tasks when requirements change, because we all know that requirements change often.

So far in this chapter, we have looked at protocols from a coding point of view. In this final section, we will look at protocols from a design point of view.

Designing and developing with protocols

With protocol-oriented programming, we should always begin our design with the protocols, but how should we design these protocols? In the object-oriented programming world, we have superclasses that contain all of the base requirements for the subclasses.

In the protocol-oriented programming world, we use protocols instead of superclasses, and it is preferable to break our requirements into smaller, very specific protocols rather than having bigger monolithic protocols. In this section, we will look at how we can separate our requirements into smaller, very specific protocols and then use protocol composition to add the requirements to our types.

In this section, we will be demonstrating how to define property requirements in our protocols. In Chapter 5, *Let's Extend Some Types*, we will show you how to add functionality to all types that conform to a protocol using protocol extensions.

For the example in this section, we will model something that my daughters and I really enjoy doing, namely Tae Kwon Do. As we progress through the Tae Kwon Do ranks, we are required to take tests to see if we know the requirements for our belt color and rank. If we pass the tests, we are promoted to the next belt color and/or rank. Each of these belt colors and ranks has different testing requirements. For example, to test for a yellow belt we need to do our form, one step, and focus pad drills, but to test for a blue belt we need to do our form, focus pad drills, board breaks, and sparring.

The different testing areas are as follows:

- Forms
- Focus pad drills
- One steps
- Board breaks
- Sparring

If we were going to model the different testing requirements in an object-oriented way, we would start off by creating a superclass that contained all of the testing areas, even though not all subclasses will need all of the testing areas. We would then create subclasses of this superclass that would contain the individual requirements for each of the tests. Before we see how we would do this in an object-oriented way, let's create two enumerations that will define the different belt colors and ranks. We will also create a type alias that will define the board break requirements. The following code shows how we would define these:

```
enum TKDBeltColors: Int {
    case White, Yellow, Orage, Green, Blue, Purple, Red, FirstDegreeBlack,
SecondDegreeBlack, ThirdDegreeBlack, ForthDegreeBlack
```

```
}

enum TKDColorRank: Int {
    case NoRank, Probationary, Decided, Intermediate, Senior
}

typealias BoardBreak = (name: String, required: Bool)
```

For the board breaking requirements, we have to break a certain number of boards (depending on the rank) from a list of possible techniques. Some of these techniques are required techniques while others are optional. Our `BoardBreak` associated type is a tuple that contains a string value that specifies the technique and a Boolean value that specifies whether that technique is required or not.

Now that we have defined our enumerations and associated type, let's design the class hierarchy that will model our different testing requirements. We will start off by creating a superclass named `TKDTestingRequirements`, and all of the other Tae Kwon Do testing classes will be subclasses of this superclass:

```
class TKDTestingRequirements {
    var color = TKDBeltColors.White
    var rank = TKDColorRank.NoRank
    var formName = ""
    var focusPadDrills = [String]()
    var focusPadMissesAllowed = 2
    var sparringRoundsRequired = 0
    var boardBreaksRequired = 0
    var boardBreaks: [BoardBreak]?
    var oneStepsNumbers: [Int]?
}
```

In the `TKDTestingRequirements` class, we defined all possible requirements that we may have for testing. This includes requirements such as the one steps, which are only requirements for the white and yellow belt testing. All other belt and rank classes will need to set the `oneStepsNumbers` property to `nil`, indicating that it is not required for testing.

We can then subclass the `TKDTestingRequirements` class to define the requirements for our tests. As examples, the following classes define the requirements for the white and senior green belt tests:

```
class WhiteBelt: TKDTestingRequirements {
    override init () {
        super.init()
        color = TKDBeltColors.White
        rank = TKDColorRank.NoRank
        formName = "Chon-Ji"
```

```
            oneStepsNumbers = [1,2,3]
            focusPadDrills = ["Reverse Punch", "Number 1 Front Kick"]
            focusPadMissesAllowed = 2
            boardBreaksRequired = 0
            sparringRoundsRequired = 0
        }
    }

    class GreenBeltSenior: TKDTestingRequirements {
        override init() {
            super.init()
            color = TKDBeltColors.Green
            rank = TKDColorRank.NoRank
            formName = "Do-San"
            focusPadDrills = ["Back Fist", "Number 2 Crescent"]
            focusPadMissesAllowed = 2
            boardBreaks = [(name:"Hammer Fist", required: false),
                           (name:"Front Kick", required: false)]
            boardBreaksRequired = 1
            sparringRoundsRequired = 2
            oneStepsNumbers = nil
        }
    }
```

This design would work, and it would be fairly easy to create different classes for each of our tests. However, we are defining requirements that are not necessary for all of our testing; this is not an optimal design. As an example, we are setting the boardBreaksRequired and sparringRoundsRequired properties to 0 in the WhiteBelt class. Wouldn't it be nice if we only needed to define the requirements that are necessary for the particular test? With protocol-oriented programming, we can. Let's redesign this solution in a protocol-oriented way.

With protocol-oriented programming, instead of putting all of the requirements into a single type, as we did with the object-oriented example, we separate the requirements into multiple smaller protocols. Each of these protocols will contain the requirements for a specific testing area. For our example, the requirements are the individual testing areas:

- Forms
- Focus pad drills
- One steps
- Board breaks
- Sparring

With object-oriented programming, a class can only inherit from a single superclass; therefore, we need to put all of our requirements into a single monolithic superclass. With protocol composition we are able to let a single type adopt multiple protocols. This way, we can break our requirements into multiple smaller protocols. This allows us to implement only the requirements necessary for our type.

Our testing area protocols would look such as this:

```
protocol TKDRankProtocol {
    var color: TKDBeltColors {get}
    var rank: TKDColorRank {get}
}
protocol BoardBreakProtocol {
    var boardBreaks: [BoardBreak] {get}
    var boardBreaksRequired: Int {get}
}

protocol FormProtocol {
    var formName: String {get}
}

protocol FocusPadProtocol {
    var focusPadDrills: [String] {get}
    var focusPadMissesAllowed: Int {get}
}

protocol OneStepsProtocol {
    var oneStepsNumbers: [Int] {get}
}

protocol SparringProtocol {
    var sparringRoundsRequired: Int {get}
}
```

Each of these protocols only contains the requirements for its specific testing areas. When we design our applications, it is important to separate our requirements into smaller protocols like this so we do not have to implement requirements that do not pertain to our type.

We can now adopt these protocols, as shown in the next example:

```
struct WhiteBelt: TKDRankProtocol, FormProtocol, OneStepsProtocol,
  FocusPadProtocol {
    let color = TKDBeltColors.White
    let rank = TKDColorRank.NoRank
    let formName = "Chon-Ji"
    let oneStepsNumbers = [1,2,3]
```

```
        let focusPadDrills = ["Reverse Punch", "Number 1 Front Kick"]
        let focusPadMissesAllowed = 2
}

struct GreenBeltSenior: TKDRankProtocol, FormProtocol,
            BoardBreakProtocol, FocusPadProtocol, SparringProtocol {
    let color = TKDBeltColors.Green
    let rank = TKDColorRank.NoRank
    let formName = "Do-San"
    let focusPadDrills = ["Back Fist", "Number 2 Crescent"]
    let focusPadMissesAllowed = 2
    let boardBreaks = [(name:"Hammer Fist", required: false),
                        (name:"Front Kick", required: false)]
    let boardBreaksRequired = 1
    let sparringRoundsRequired = 2
}
```

For each of these types, we only adopt the requirements that are needed; therefore, we are not implementing any unnecessary requirements. This is a more optimal design, and should be preferred to the object-oriented design that we saw earlier in this section.

We can then use the is and as keywords as described in the *Type casting with protocols* section of this chapter to check whether an instance conforms to a specific type. Checking for and casting to a specific protocol takes the same form as checking for and casting to a specific type.

Summary

While protocol-oriented programming is about so much more than just the protocol, it would be impossible to have the protocol-oriented programming paradigm without the protocol. We can think of the protocol as the backbone of protocol-oriented programming. Therefore, it is important to fully understand the protocol in order to properly implement protocol-oriented programming.

In this chapter, we looked at how to implement protocols in our application. We also looked at many of the features that protocols offer. We concluded this chapter with two sections on how to properly use protocols.

Extensions are the final piece of the protocol-oriented programming puzzle. In the next chapter, we will look at how we can use extensions in Swift.

5
Lets Extend Some Types

Back in the early 90's, when the primary language that I developed in was C, I had numerous custom libraries that contained functionality that was not part of the standard C library. I found these libraries extremely useful because I tended to use the functionality they provided in most of my projects. This functionality included things such as converting the first letter of a string to uppercase or converting a double value to a currency string (two digits after the decimal point and a currency symbol). Having libraries such as these is extremely useful because there is always functionality that we find useful that is not included in the standard library of the language we are developing in. I usually implemented this extra functionality in C with global functions. In more modern object-oriented languages, we can implement this functionality by sub-classing the class we wish to add the functionality to, but in Swift we can use extensions to add this functionality to existing types without the need to use global functions or sub-classing. To make extensions even more useful, Apple gave us the ability to extend protocols, which lets us add functionality to any type that adopts a protocol.

We will learn the following in this chapter:

- How to extend structures, classes, and enumerations
- How to extend protocols
- How to use extensions in a real-world example

Extensions are one of the most useful features in the Swift language. They allow us to add functionality to an existing type even if we do not have the source code for the type. Protocol extensions are arguably one of the most exciting features of protocol-oriented programming. If you are not familiar with protocol extensions, you may be wondering how we can add functionality to a protocol when protocols do not contain any functionality. We will see how to use protocol extensions later in this chapter and see why they are so exciting. First, however, let's look at what extensions are and how to extend classes, structures, and enumerations.

With extensions, we can add the following items to an existing type:

- Computed properties
- Instance and type methods
- Convenience initializers
- Subscripts

One drawback of extensions is that we cannot override the functionality of the type we are extending. Extensions are designed to add additional functionality and are not designed as a means of changing the functionality of a type. Another thing that we cannot do with extensions is add stored properties; however, we can add computed properties.

To understand why extensions are so useful, we need to understand the problem that they are designed to solve. In most object-oriented languages, when we want to add additional functionality to an existing class, we generally subclass the class we want to add the extra functionality to. We then add the new functionality to this new sub-class. The problem with this method is that we are not actually adding the functionality to the original class; therefore, we have to change all instances of the original class which need this extra functionality, to instances of this new sub-class. With some classes, such as the NSString class, it can take a significant amount of code to create a sub-class. There is a sample Objective-C project in the downloadable code that demonstrates this.

Another problem we can run into is that we can only subclass reference types (classes). This means we are unable to subclass value types such as a structure or enumeration. What makes matters even worse is the fact that the greater part of the Swift standard library is made up of value types. Therefore, we are unable to add functionality to types from the Swift standard library by sub-classing them. Apple has also recommended that we prefer value types to reference types in our applications, which means that if we listen to Apple's recommendation, we cannot subclass the majority of our custom types.

With extensions, we are able to add new functionality directly to the types that we are extending. This means that all instances of that type automatically receive the new functionality without the need to change the type of the instance. We are also able to extend both reference and value types, which includes protocols. As we will see later in this chapter, the ability to extend protocols is one of the things that make protocol-oriented programming possible.

Let's begin by looking at how we extend types such as structures, enumerations, and classes.

Defining an extension

An extension is defined by using the `extension` keyword followed by the name of the type you are extending. We then put the functionality that we are adding to the type between curly brackets. The following example shows how to define an extension:

```
extension String {
    // Add functionality here
}
```

The previous example would add an extension to the `String` type from the Swift standard library. Since we can extend any type, we can use extensions to add functionality to types from the Swift standard library, types from frameworks/libraries, or our own custom types. While we can use extensions to add functionality to our own custom types, it is usually better to add the functionality directly to the type itself. The reason for this is that our code is easier to maintain if all of the functionality (code) for our custom types is located together.

If we are adding functionality to a framework and we have the code for that framework, it is still better to add the functionality with an extension rather than changing the code within the framework itself. The reason for this is that, if we add the functionality directly to the code within the framework, when we get newer versions of the framework, our changes will be overwritten. Newer versions of the framework will not overwrite our extensions as long as we do not put them in a file that belongs to the framework.

Let's see how we can add functionality to a standard Swift type using an extension. The following code extends the `String` type to add a method that returns an optional value that contains either the first character of the string or a `nil`, if the string is empty:

```
extension String {
    func getFirstChar() -> Character? {
        guard characters.count > 0 else {
            return nil
        }
        return self[startIndex]
    }
}
```

Once we add this extension to our application, all instances of the String type can take advantage of the new functionality. There is also nothing special that needs to be done to access the functionality; instances of the String type do not know or care whether the functionality came from the original implementation of the type or from an extension. The following example shows how we use the getFirstChar() method:

```
var myString = "This is a test"
print(myString.getFirstChar())
```

The previous example will print the character T to the console. It is just as easy to add other functionality such as subscripts to existing types. The following example shows how we would add a subscript to our String extension that accepts a range operator and returns a substring with the characters defined by the range operator:

```
extension String {
    func getFirstChar() -> Character? {
        guard characters.count > 0 else {
            return nil
        }
        return self[startIndex]
    }

    subscript (r: CountableClosedRange<Int>) -> String {
        get {
            let start = index(self.startIndex, offsetBy:r.lowerBound)
            let end = index(self.startIndex, offsetBy:r.upperBound)
            return substring(with: start..<end)
        }
    }
}
```

In Chapter 2, *Our Type Choices*, we mentioned that types that are normally implemented as primitives in other languages are implemented as named types in Swift. These include types that represent numbers, characters, and Boolean values. Since they are implemented as named types, we are also able to extend them as we would any other type. As an example, if we wanted to extend the Int type to add a method that would return the value of the integer squared, we could do it with an extension like this:

```
extension Int {
    func squared() -> Int {
        return self * self
    }
}
```

We could then use this extension to get the value of any integer squared, as shown in the following example:

```
var i = 21
print(i.squared())
```

Another example would be to extend the `Double` type to add a method that would convert the value of the double to a `String` type representing the value as a currency. This method would round the number to two decimal places and add a currency symbol. The following code demonstrates how we could do this:

```
extension Double {
    func currencyString() -> String {
        let divisor = pow(10.0, 2.0)
        let num = (self * divisor).rounded() / divisor
        return "$\(num)"
    }
}
```

We cannot add stored properties with extensions; however; we can add computed properties. Earlier in this section, we added a method named `squared()` to the `Int` type. We could have implemented this functionality as a computed property, as shown in the following example:

```
extension Int {
    var squared: Int {
        return self * self
    }
}
```

Now that we have seen how to extend a standard type such as classes, enumerations, or structures, let's see what protocol extensions are all about.

Protocol extensions

Protocols, like other types, can be extended. Protocol extensions can be used to provide common functionality to all types that conform to a particular protocol. This gives us the ability to add functionality to any type that conforms to a protocol rather than adding the functionality to each individual type or through a global function. Protocol extensions, like regular extensions, also give us the ability to add functionality to types that we do not have the source code for.

Protocol-oriented programming and frameworks such as **GameplayKit** would not be possible without protocol extensions. Without protocol extensions, if we wanted to add specific functionality to a group of types that conformed to a protocol, we would have to add the functionality to each of the types. If we were using reference types (classes), we could create a class hierarchy, but that is not possible for value types. Apple has stated that we should prefer value types to reference types and with protocol extensions we have the ability to add common functionality to a group of values and/or reference types that conform to a specific protocol, without having to implement that functionality in all types.

Let's see what protocol extensions can do for us. The Swift standard library provides a protocol named `Collection` (https://developer.apple.com/reference/swift/collect ion). This protocol inherits from the `Indexable` and `Sequence` protocols and it is adopted by all of Swift's standard collection types, for example, `Dictionary` and `Array`.

Let's say that we wanted to add the functionality to all types that conform to the `Collection` protocol. This new functionality would shuffle the items in a collection or return only the items whose index number is an even number. We could very easily add this functionality by extending the `Collection` protocol, as shown in the following code:

```
extension Collection {
    func evenElements() -> [Generator.Element] {

        var index = startIndex
        var result: [Generator.Element] = []
        var i = 0
        repeat {
            if i % 2 == 0 {
                result.append(self[index])
            }
            index = self.index(after: index)
            i += 1
        } while (index != endIndex)
        return result
    }

    func shuffle() -> [Generator.Element] {
        return sorted(){ left, right in
            return arc4random() < arc4random()
        }
    }
}
```

Notice that when we extend a protocol, we use the same syntax and format that we use when we extend other types. We use the `extension` keyword followed by the name of the protocol that we are extending. We then put the functionality we are adding between the curly brackets. Now every type that conforms to the `Collection` protocol will receive both the `evenElements()` and `shuffle()` functions. The following code shows how we would use these functions with an array:

```
var origArray = [1,2,3,4,5,6,7,8,9,10]

var newArray = origArray.evenElements()
var ranArray = origArray.shuffle()
```

In the previous code, the `newArray` array will contain the elements 1, 3, 5, 7, and 9 because those elements have index numbers that are even (we are looking at the index number, not the value of the element). The `ranArray` array will contain the same elements as the `origArray`, but the order will be shuffled.

Protocol extensions are great for adding functionality to a group of types without the need to add the code to each of the individual types; however, it is important to know what types conform to the protocol we are extending. In the previous example, we extended the `Collection` protocol by adding the `evenElements()` and `shuffle()` methods to all types that conform to the protocol. One of the types that conform to this protocol is the `Dictionary` type. However, the `Dictionary` type is an unordered collection; therefore, the `evenElements()` method will not work as expected. The following example illustrates this:

```
var origDict = [1:"One",",2:"Two",",3:"Three",",4:"Four"]"]
var returnElements = origDict.evenElements()
for item in returnElements {
    print(item)
}
```

Since the `Dictionary` type does not promise to store the items in any particular order, any of the two items could be printed to the screen in this example. The following shows one possible output from this code:

```
(2, "two")
(1, "One")
```

Another problem is that anyone who is not familiar with how the `evenElements()` method is implemented may expect the `returnElements` instance to be of the `Dictionary` type since the original collection is a `Dictionary` type; however, it is actually an instance of the `Array` type. This can cause some confusion; therefore, we need to be careful when we extend a protocol to make sure the functionality we are adding works as expected for all types that conform to the protocol. In the case of the `shuffle()` and `evenElements()` methods, we might have been better served to add the functionality as an extension directly to the `Array` type rather than the `Collection` protocol; however, there is another way. We can add constraints to our extensions that will limit the types that receive the functionality defined in an extension.

In order for a type to receive the functionality defined in a protocol extension, it must satisfy all constraints defined within the protocol extension. A constraint is added after the name of the protocol that we are extending using the `where` keyword. The following example shows how we would add a constraint to our `Collection` extension:

```
extension Collection where Self: ExpressibleByArrayLiteral {
  //Extension code here
}
```

In the `Collection` protocol extensions in the previous example, only types that also conform to the `ExpressibleByArrayLiteral` protocol (`https://developer.apple.com/reference/swift/expressiblebyarrayliteral`) will receive the functionality defined in the extension. Since the `Dictionary` type does not conform to the `ExpressibleByArrayLiteral` protocol, it will not receive the functionality defined within the protocol extension.

We could also use constraints to specify that our `Collection` protocol extension only applies to a collection whose elements conform to a specific protocol. In the following example, we use constraints to make sure that the elements in the collection conform to the `Comparable` protocol. This may be necessary if the functionality that we are adding relies on the ability to compare two or more elements in the collection. We could add this constraint as follows:

```
extension Collection where Iterator.Element: Comparable {
   // Add functionality here
}
```

Constraints give us the ability to limit which types receive the functionality defined in the extension. One thing that we need to be careful of is using protocol extensions when we should actually be extending an individual type. Protocol extensions should be used when we want to add functionality to a group of types. If we are trying to add the functionality to a single type, we should look to extend that individual type.

In Chapter 4, *All About the Protocol*, we created a series of protocols that defined the Tae Kwon Do testing areas. Let's see how we could extend the TKDRank protocol from that example to add the ability to store which testing areas the student passed and which areas they failed. The following code is for the original TKDRank protocol from Chapter 4, *All About the Protocol*:

```
protocol TKDRank {
    var color: TKDBeltColors {get}
    var rank: TKDColorRank {get}
}
```

We will begin by adding an instance of the Dictionary type to our protocol. This Dictionary type will store the results of our tests. The following example shows what the new TKDRank protocol will look like:

```
protocol TKDRank {
    var color: TKDBeltColors {get}
    var rank: TKDColorRank {get}
    var passFailTests: [String:Bool] {get set}
}
```

We can now extend the TKDRank protocol to add a method that we can use to set whether the student passes or fails an individual test. The following code shows how we would do this:

```
extension TKDRank {
    mutating func setPassFail(testName: String, pass: Bool) {
        passFailTests[testName] = pass
    }
}
```

Now, any type that conforms to the TKDRank protocol will have the setPassFail() method automatically.

Now that we have seen how to use extensions and protocol extensions, let's look at a real-world example. In this example, we will show how to create a text validation framework.

Text validation

In numerous apps, across multiple platforms (iOS, Android, and Windows), I have been tasked to validate user input either after the user has entered it or as it is entered. This validation can be done very easily with regular expressions; however, we do not want various regular expression strings littered throughout our code. We can solve this problem by creating different classes or structures that contain the validation code. The question is; how would we organize these types to make them easy to use and maintain? Prior to protocol extensions in Swift, I would have used protocols to define the validation requirements and would then create a type that conforms to the protocol for each validation type needed.

Prior to looking at how we would accomplish this text validation, let's take a quick look at what regular expressions are and how we would use them in Swift. A regular expression (also known as **regex**) is a special text string that is used to describe a search or matching pattern. The regular expression string, also known as a pattern, consists of one or more characters, operators, or constructs. Regular expressions are very useful when searching for a string for a particular pattern or (as we use it here) validating a string.

Regular expressions are not unique to Swift. Almost all modern languages have a way to use regular expressions. Whole books have been written about regular expressions, so in this section, we will give a very brief introduction with enough information for you to understand the examples in this chapter.

In its simplest form, a regular expression is a string of characters such as abc or 12345. Using a regular expression such as this will match the pattern within a string, as shown in the following examples:

Regex	Matches	Description
abc	xyzabcxyzabc	Matches the string abc
12345	1234567890	Matches the string 12345

We can also define character sets using square brackets ([ ]). Character sets will match one character in the string to any character within the set. To define the set, we can use a string of characters, as shown in the last example, or we can use the minus sign (–) operator to specify a range:

Regex	Matches	Description
[abc]	xyzabcxyz	Matches any character in the set abc
[a-zA-Z]	xyzabcxyz	Matches any lower or uppercase letter

We use curly brackets ({ }) to specify the amount of repetition so we can match more than one character. For example, if we used {2,5} then that would mean we want to match at least 2 characters, but no more than 5 characters:

Regex	Matches	Description
[a-z]{2,5}	xyzabcxyz	Matches 2 to 5 lowercase letters
[a-z0-9]{2,5}	xyzabcxyz	Matches 2 to 5 lowercase letters or numbers

The caret (^) at the beginning means we want to match at the beginning and the dollar sign ($) means match at the end. We can use these two special characters to match a full string. For example, the ^[a-z]{0,5}$ pattern will match a string only if there are between 0 and 5 lowercase letters. The match will fail if there are any other characters besides lowercase letters or more than five characters:

Regex	Matches	Description
^[a-z]{2,5}$	xyzabcxyz	Fails more than five characters
[a-z0-9]{0,5}	xyz12	Matches five lowercase or number characters

Finally, let's look at some additional special characters within regular expressions. These are characters that need to be escaped using the backslash (\) and have special meaning:

Character	Definition
.	The dot matches any single character
\n	Matches a newline character
\t	Matches a tab
\d	Matches a digit [0-9]
\D	Matches a non-digit
\w	Matches an alphanumeric character [a-zA-Z0-9]
\W	Matches a non-alphanumeric character
\s	Matches a whitespace character
\S	Matches a non-whitespace character

There is a lot more to regular expressions than we have just seen. In this section, we only gave enough information to help you understand the text validation examples in this chapter. If you plan on using regular expressions on a regular (pun intended) basis, I would suggest reading more about them.

Now let's look at how we would develop our validation framework without protocol extensions. We will begin by defining a `TextValidation` protocol that will define the requirements for any type that we will use for text validation. This will allow us to use the `TextValidation` protocol in place of implementation types. If you recall, this is a form of polymorphism:

```
protocol TextValidation {

    var regExMatchingString: String {get}
    var regExFindMatchString: String {get}
    var validationMessage: String {get}
    func validateString(str: String) -> Bool
    func getMatchingString(str: String) -> String?
}
```

In this protocol, we define three properties and two methods that any type that conforms to the `TextValidation` protocol must implement. The three properties are:

- `regExMatchingString`: Regular expression string used to verify that the input string contains only valid characters.
- `regExFindMatchString`: Regular expression string used to retrieve a new string from the input string that contains only valid characters. This regular expression is generally used when we need to validate the input in real time, as the user enters information, because it will remove all characters starting with the first invalid characters to the end of the string.
- `validationMessage`: This is the error message to display if the input string contained non-valid characters.

The two methods for this protocol are:

- `validateString`: This method will return `true` if the input string contains only valid characters. The `regExMatchingString` property will be used in this method to perform the match.
- `getMatchingString`: This method will return a new string that contains only valid characters. This method is generally used when we need to validate the input in real time, as the user enters information, because it will remove all characters starting with the first invalid characters. We will use the `regExFindMatchString` property in this method to retrieve the new string.

Now let's see how we would create a class that conforms to this protocol. The following class would be used to verify that the input string contains 0 to 10 alpha characters:

```
class AlphabeticValidation1: TextValidation {
    static let sharedInstance = AlphabeticValidation1()
    private init(){}
    let regExFindMatchString = "^[a-zA-Z]{0,10}"
    let validationMessage = "Can only contain Alpha characters"
    var regExMatchingString: String { get {
        return regExFindMatchString + "$"
        }
    }
    func validateString(str: String) -> Bool {
        if let _ = str.range(of: regExMatchingString, options:
                    .regularExpression){
            return true
        } else {
            return false
        }
    }
    func getMatchingString(str: String) -> String? {
        if let newMatch = str.range(of: regExFindMatchString, options:
                    .regularExpression) {
            return str.substring(with: newMatch)
        } else {
            return nil
        }
    }
}
```

In this implementation, the regExFindMatchString and validationMessage properties are stored properties and the regExMatchingString property is a computed property. We also implement the validateString() and getMatchingString() methods within the class to conform to the protocol.

Normally, we would have several different types that conform to the TextValidation protocol where each one would validate a different type of input. As we can see from the AlphabeticValidation1 class, there is quite a bit of code involved with each validation type. A lot of the code would need to be duplicated for each validation type. This is not ideal. However, if we wanted to avoid creating a class hierarchy with a superclass containing the duplicate code, we would have no other choice. Protocol extensions give us a better option. Let's take a look at how we would implement our text validation types with protocol extensions.

With protocol extensions, we need to think about the code a little differently. The big difference is that we do not need, nor want to define, everything in the protocol. With standard protocols or when we use a class hierarchy, all methods and properties that we want to access using the interface provided by the generic superclass or protocol type have to be defined within the superclass or protocol. With protocol extensions, it is actually preferable for us to not define a computed property or method in the protocol if we are going to implement it within the protocol extension. Therefore, when we rewrite our text validation types with protocol extensions, the TextValidation protocol would be greatly simplified and would look like this:

```
protocol TextValidation {
    var regExFindMatchString: String {get}
    var validationMessage: String {get}
}
```

In the original TextValidation protocol, we defined three properties and two methods. As we can see in this new protocol, we are only defining two properties. Now that we have our TextValidation defined, let's create a protocol extension where we implement the other two methods and the computed property:

```
extension TextValidation {
    var regExMatchingString: String { get {
        return regExFindMatchString + "$"
        }
    }
    func validateString(str: String) -> Bool {
        if let _ = str.range(of: regExMatchingString, options:
                    .regularExpression){
            return true
        } else {
            return false
        }
    }
    func getMatchingString(str: String) -> String? {
        if let newMatch = str.range(of: regExFindMatchString, options:
                        .regularExpression){
            return str.substring(with: newMatch)
        } else {
            return nil
        }
    }
}
```

In the `TextValidation` protocol extension, we implement the two methods and the computed property that were defined in the original `TextValidation` protocol, but not defined in the new one.

Now that we have created our protocol and protocol extension, we are able to define our text validation types. In the following code, we define three classes that we will use to validate text:

```
class AlphabeticValidation: TextValidation {
    static let sharedInstance = AlphabeticValidation()
    private init(){}
    let regExFindMatchString = "^[a-zA-Z]{0,10}"
    let validationMessage = "Can only contain Alpha characters"
}

class AlphaNumericValidation: TextValidation {
    static let sharedInstance = AlphaNumericValidation()
    private init(){}
    let regExFindMatchString = "^[a-zA-Z0-9]{0,15}"
    let validationMessage = "Can only contain Alpha Numeric characters"
}


class DisplayNameValidation: TextValidation {
    static let sharedInstance = DisplayNameValidation()
    private init(){}
    let regExFindMatchString = "^[\\s?[a-zA-Z0-9\\-_\\s]]{0,15}"
    let validationMessage = "Display Name can contain only contain
Alphanumeric Characters"
}
```

In each of the text validation classes, we create a static constant and a private initiator so we can use the class as a singleton. For more information on the singleton pattern please see *The singleton design pattern* section of `Chapter 7`, *Adopting Design Patterns in Swift*.

After we define the singleton pattern, all we do in each type is set the values for the `regExFindMatchString` and the `validationMessage` properties. Now we have virtually no duplicate code between the types except the code to implement the singleton pattern. Even if we could, we would not want to define the singleton code in the protocol extension because we would not want to force that pattern on all conforming types. We can also see that we are able to define these three classes with less code than it took to define the one class without protocol extensions.

We could use these validation classes as follows:

```
var myString1 = "abcxyz"
var myString2 = "abc123"

var validation = AlphabeticValidation.sharedInstance

validation.validateString(str: myString1)
validation.validateString(str: myString2)

validation.getMatchingString(str: myString1)
validation.getMatchingString(str: myString2)
```

In this example, we create two String types, each containing a different string value. We then get the shared instance of the AlphabeticValidation type. We use the validateString() method of the AlphabeticValidation instance to validate the strings, which verifies that the whole string matches the regular expression pattern defined in the AlphabeticValidation instance. We then use the getMatchingString() method of the AlphabeticValidation instance to return a new string that contains only the valid characters defined in the regular expression pattern.

The validateString() method returns a true value for the myString1 instance because the value of myString1 matches the regular expression pattern; however, it returns a false value for the myString2 instances because their value contains numbers that do not match the ^[a-zA-Z]{0,10} regular expression pattern defined in the AlphabeticValidation type.

The getMatchingString() method returns the full value of myString1 because the value matches the regular expression pattern defined in the AlphabeticValidation type. However, for the value of the myString2 instance, it only returns an instance of the string type that contains the value of abc because that is the only part of the myString2 value that matches the pattern.

Let's look at how we could use the text validation code to validate input into a UITextField in an iOS application. We will not go through how to add a UITextField in a storyboard or wiring up the UITextField with our backend code, but you can take a look at the sample application included with the downloadable code for this book to see how it all works together. The example will have three text fields named: alphaTextField, alphaNumericTextField, and displayNameTextField. We will want to create a Dictionary object that maps the UITextField instances to the validation classes as follows:

```
var validators = [UITextField: TextValidation]()
```

We could then populate the `validators` dictionary as shown in the following code:

```
validators[alphaTextField!] = AlphabeticValidation.sharedInstance

validators[alphaNumericTextField!] = AlphaNumericValidation.sharedInstance

validators[displayNameTextField!] = DisplayNameValidation.sharedInstance
```

We can now set the `Editing Changed` event of the text fields to a single method. This method would look as follows:

```
@IBAction func keyPressed(textField: UITextField) {
    if let validator = validators[textField] where
!validator.validateString(textField.text!) {
    textField.text = validator.getMatchingString(textField.text!)
        messageLabel?.text = validator.validationMessage
    }
}
```

In this method, we use the `if let validator = validators[textField]` statement to retrieve the validator for the particular text field and then we use the `where` `!validator.validateString(textField.text!)` statement to validate the string that the user has entered. If the string fails validation, we use the `getMatchingString()` method to update the text in the text field by removing all characters from the input string, starting with the first invalid character, and then display the error message from the text validation class.

In the downloadable code for this book, you will find a sample project that demonstrates how to use text validation types.

Summary

In this chapter, we looked at extensions and protocol extensions. In the original version of Swift, we were able to use extensions to extend structures, classes, and enumerations, but since Swift 2, we have also been able to use extensions to extend protocols.

Without protocol extensions, protocol-oriented programming would not be possible, but we need to make sure that we use protocol extensions where appropriate and do not try to use them where regular extensions should be used.

In the next chapter, we will look at the final piece of the protocol-oriented puzzle and one that we have not mentioned much in this book so far: Generics.

6
Working with Generics

I received a lot of feedback about protocol-oriented programming after the first version of this book was released. Almost all of this feedback was very positive; however, there was one conversation that I had, with one of the smartest people that I have had the privilege to meet, about what protocol-oriented programming was. One of the comments that he made was that I should not forget about generic programming. The conversation that we had about generic programming really stuck with me and when I had the opportunity to write the new version of this book, I took that opportunity to include this chapter on generics.

What we will learn in this chapter:

- What generics are
- How to create generic functions
- How to create generic types
- How to design very flexible and reusable types with protocols and generics

Generics allow us to write very flexible and reusable code that avoids duplication. With a type safe language, such as Swift, we often need to write functions or types that are valid for multiple types. For example, we might need to write a function that swaps the values of two variables; however, we may want this function to swap two `String` types, two `Int` types, and two `Double` types. Without generics, we will need to write three separate functions; however, with generics, we can write one generic function to provide the swap functionality for different types. Generics allow us to tell a function or type—*I know Swift is a type-safe language, but I do not know the type that will be needed yet. I will give you a placeholder for now and will let you know what type to enforce at runtime.*

Whether you realize it or not, generics play a very large part of every program written in Swift because generics play such a large part in the Swift language itself. In fact, much of the Swift standard library is built with generic code. We can look at arrays as an example of where generics are used in the Swift standard library. Generics allow us to create an array that contains `Int` values, `String` values, or instances of any other type.

Optionals are another example of where generics are used in the Swift language. The optional type is defined as an enumeration with two possible values, `None` and `Some(T)`, where `T` is the associated value of the appropriate type. If we set the optional to `nil`, then it will have a value of `None`, and if we set a value for the optional then it will have a value of `Some` with an associated value of the appropriate type. Internally, an optional is defined as follows:

```
enum Optional<T> {
   case None
   case Some(T)
}
```

Here, `T` is the type to associate with the optional. The `T` symbol is used to define a generic. As we will see later in this chapter, we are not limited to the `T` symbol, but for most of the examples in this chapter, we will use either the `T` or `E` symbol to represent a generic because those are the standard symbols used in most documentation.

In Swift, we have the ability to define both generic functions and generic types. Let's start by looking at how we would create a generic function.

Generic functions

To fully understand generics we need to understand the problem that they are designed to solve. Let's say that we wanted to create functions that swapped the values of two variables (as described in the first part of this chapter); however, for our application, we have a need to swap two `Int` types, two `Double` types, and two `String` types. Without generics, this would require us to write the following three functions:

```
func swapInts (a: inout Int,b: inout Int) {
    let tmp = a
    a = b
    b = tmp
}

func swapDoubles(a: inout Double,b: inout Double) {
    let tmp = a
    a = b
```

```
        b = tmp
    }

    func swapStrings(a: inout String, b: inout String) {
        let tmp = a
        a = b
        b = tmp
    }
```

With these three functions, we can swap the original values of two `Int` types, two `Double` types, and two `String` types. Now, let's say as we develop our application further, we find out that we also need to swap the values of two `UInt32` types, two `Float` types, or even a couple of custom types. We might easily end up with eight or nine swap functions. The worst part is each of these functions would contain duplicate code because the only difference between them is the different parameter types. While this solution does work, generics offer a much more elegant and simple solution that eliminates all of the duplicate code. Let's see how we would condense all three of the preceding functions into a single generic function:

```
    func swapGeneric<T>(a: inout T, b: inout T) {
        let tmp = a
        a = b
        b = tmp
    }
```

Let's look at how we defined the `swapGeneric(a:b:)` function. The function itself looks pretty similar to a normal function, except for the capital `T`. The capital `T`, as used in the `swapGeneric(a:b:)` function, is a placeholder type and tells Swift that we will be defining the type later. We can then use that placeholder type in place of any type definition within the parameter definitions, the return type, or the function itself. The big thing to keep in mind is that, once the placeholder is defined as a type, all the other placeholders assume that type. Therefore, any variable or constant defined with that placeholder must conform to that type.

There is nothing special about the capital `T`, we could use any valid identifier in place of `T`. The following definitions are perfectly valid:

```
    func swapGeneric <G>(a: inout G, b: inout G) {
      //Statements
    }

    func swapGeneric <xyz>(a: inout xyz, b: inout xyz) {
      //Statements
    }
```

In most documentation, generic placeholders are defined with either T (for type) or E (for element). For standard purposes, we will use T to define generic placeholders in this chapter. It is also good practice to use T to define a generic placeholder within our code so the placeholder is easily recognized when we are looking at the code at a later time.

Let's look at how we would call a generic function. The following code will swap two integers:

```
var a = 5
var b = 10
swapGeneric(a: &a, b: &b)

print("a:  \(a) b:  \(b)")
```

If we run this code, the output would be: a: 10 b: 5. We can see that we do not have to do anything special to call a generic function. The function infers the type from the first parameter and then sets all the remaining placeholders to that type. Now, if we needed to swap the values of two Strings, we could use the same function as follows:

```
var c = "My String 1"
var d = "My String 2"
swapGeneric(a: &c, b: &d)
print("c:  \(c) d:  \(d)")
```

We can see that we call the function in exactly the same way as we called it when we wanted to swap two integers. One thing that we cannot do is pass two different types into the swapGeneric() function because we defined only one generic placeholder. If we attempt to run the following code, we will receive an error:

```
var a = 5
var c = "My String 1"
swapGeneric(a: &a, b: &c)
```

The error that we would receive is; cannot convert value of type 'String' to expected argument type 'Int', which tells us that we are attempting to use a String type where an Int type is expected. The reason the function is looking for an Int value is that the first parameter that we pass into the function is an Int type; therefore, all of the generic types in the function defined with the T placeholder became Int types.

If we need to use multiple generic types, we can create multiple placeholders by separating them with commas. The following example shows how to define multiple placeholders for a single function:

```
func testGeneric<T,E>(a:T, b:E) {
    print("\(a) \(b)")
}
```

In this example, we are defining two generic placeholders, T and E. In this case, we can set the T placeholder to one type and the E placeholder to a different type.

This function will accept parameters of different types; however, since they are of different types, we would be unable to swap the values. There are also other limitations on generics as well. For example, we may think that the following generic function would be valid; however, we would receive an error if we tried to implement it:

```
func genericEqual<T>(a: T, b: T) -> Bool{
    return a == b
}
```

The error that we receive is binary operator '==' cannot be applied to two 'T' operands. Since the type of the arguments is unknown at the time the code is compiled, Swift does not know if it is able to use the equal operator on the types, which causes the error to be thrown. We might think that this is a limit that would make generics hard to use; however, we have a way to tell Swift that we expect the type will have certain functionality. This is done with type constraints.

Type constraints with generics

A type constraint specifies that a generic type must inherit from a specific class or conform to a particular protocol. This allows us to use the methods or properties defined by the parent class or protocol with the generic types. Let's look at how to use type constraints by rewriting the genericEqual() function to use the Comparable protocol:

```
func testGenericComparable<T: Comparable>(a: T, b: T) -> Bool{
    return a >= b
}
```

To specify the type constraint, we put the class or protocol constraint after the generic placeholder, where the generic placeholder and the constraint are separated by a colon. This new function works as we might expect, and it will compare the values of the two parameters and return `true` if they are equal or `false` if they are not.

We can declare multiple constraints just like we declare multiple generic types. The following example shows how to declare two generic types with different constraints:

```
func testFunction<T: MyClass, E: MyProtocol>(a: T, b: E) {
}
```

In this function, the type defined by the T placeholder must inherit from the MyClass class, and the type defined by the E placeholder must implement the MyProtocol protocol. Now that we have looked at generic functions and type constraints, let's take a look at generic types.

Generic types

A generic type is a class, structure, or enumeration that can work with any type, just like Swift arrays and optionals can work with any type. When we create an instance of our generic type, we specify the type that the instance will work with. Once a type is defined, it cannot be changed for that instance.

To demonstrate how to create a generic type, let's create a simple List class. This class will use a Swift array as the backend storage and will let us add items or retrieve values from the list.

Let's begin by seeing how to define our generic list type:

```
class List<T> {
}
```

The preceding code defines the generic list type. We can see that we use the <T> tag to define a generic placeholder, just like we did when we defined a generic function. This T placeholder can then be used anywhere within the type instead of a concrete type definition.

To create an instance of this type, we would need to define the type of items that our list will hold. The following examples show how to create instances of the generic list type for various types:

```
var stringList = List<String>()
var intList = List<Int>()
var customList = List<MyObject>()
```

The preceding example creates three instances of the List class. The stringList instance can be used with String types, the intList instance can be used with Int types, and the customList instance can be used with instances of the MyObject type.

We are not limited to using generics only with classes. We can also define structures and enumerations as generic types. The following examples show how to define a generic structure and a generic enumeration:

```
struct GenericStruct<T> {
}

enum GenericEnum<T> {
}
```

The next step in our List class is to add the backend storage array. The items that are stored in this array need to be of the same type as we define when we initiate the class; therefore, we will use the T placeholder for the array's definition. The following code shows the List class with an array named items:

```
class List<T> {
    var items = [T]()
}
```

Now, we will need to add the add(item:) method that will be used to add an item to the list. We will use the T placeholder within the method declaration to define that the item parameter will be of the same type as we declared when we initiated the class. Therefore, if we create an instance of the list type to use the String type, we would be required to use the string type as the parameter for the add(item:) method.

Here is the code for the add() function:

```
func add(item: T) {
    itcms.append(item)
}
```

To create a standalone generic function, we add the <T> declaration after the function name to declare that it is a generic function. When we use a generic method within a generic type, we do not need the <T> declaration because we already specified that the type is generic for the T type when we defined it. Instead, all we need to do is to use the placeholder that we defined in the class declaration.

Now, let's add the getItemAtIndex() method that will return the item from the backend array, at the specified index:

```
func getItemAtIndex(index: Int) -> T? {
    if items.count > index {
        return items[index]
    } else {
        return nil
    }
}
```

The getItemAtIndex(index:) method accepts one argument that is the index of the item we want to retrieve. We then use the T placeholder to specify that our return type is an optional that might be of type T or might be nil. If the backend storage array contains an item at the specified index, we will return that item, otherwise, we return nil.

Now, let's look at our entire generic list class:

```
class List<T> {
    var items = [T]()
    func add(item: T) {
        items.append(item)
    }
    func getItemAtIndex(index: Int) -> T? {
        if items.count > index {
            return items[index]
        } else {
            return nil
        }
    }
}
```

As we can see, we initially defined the generic T placeholder type in the class declaration. We then used this placeholder type within our class in three places. We use it as the type for our items array, as the parameter type for the add(index:) method, and as the associated value for the optional return type in the getItemAtIndex() method.

Now, let's look at how to use the `List` class. When we use a generic type, we define the type to be used within the instance between angle brackets. The following code shows how to use the `List` class to store `String` types:

```
var list = List<String>()
list.add(item: "Hello")
list.add(item: "World")
print(list.getItemAtIndex(index: 1))
```

In this code, we start off by creating an instance of the list type called `list` and define that it will store `String` types. We then use the `add(index:)` method twice to store two items in the `list` instance. Finally, we use the `getItemAtIndex()` method to retrieve the item at index number 1, which will display `Optional(World)` to the console.

We can also define our generic types with multiple placeholder types, similar to how we use multiple placeholders in our generic methods. To use multiple placeholder types, we would separate them with commas. The following example shows how to define multiple placeholder types:

```
class MyClass<T,E>{

}
```

We then create an instance of the `MyClass` type that uses the `String` and `Int` types, such as:

```
var mc = MyClass<String, Int>()
```

Type constraints can also be used with generic types. Once again, using a type constraint for a generic type is exactly the same as using one with a generic function. The following code shows how to use a type constraint to ensure that the generic type conforms to the comparable protocol:

```
class MyClass<T: Comparable>{}
```

So far, in this chapter, we have seen how to use placeholder types with functions and types; however, this book is about protocol-oriented programming. When we declare generic types in a protocol, they are known as **associated** types.

Associated types

An associated type declares a placeholder name that can be used instead of a type within a protocol. The actual type to be used is not specified until the protocol is adopted. While creating generic functions and types, we used a very similar syntax, as we have seen throughout this chapter. Defining associated types for a protocol, however, is a little different. We specify an associated type using the `associatedtype` keyword.

Let's see how to use associated types when we define a protocol. For this example, we will create a simple protocol named `MyProtocol`:

```
protocol MyProtocol {
    associatedtype E
    var items: [E] {get set}
    mutating func add(item: E)
}
```

In this protocol, we declare an `associatedtype` named `E`. We then use that associated type as the type for the `items` array and also the parameter type for the `add(item:)` method. We can now create types that conform to this protocol by providing either a concrete type or a generic type for the associated type. Let's see how we could create a type that conforms to the `MyProtocol` protocol using a concrete type:

```
struct MyIntType: MyProtocol {
    var items: [Int] = []
    mutating func add(item: Int) {
        items.append(item)
    }
}
```

In this code, we create a type named `MyIntType` that conforms to the `MyProtocol` protocol. We then implement the `items` array and the `add(item:)` method using the `Int` type. Swift recognizes that we are using the `Int` type in place of the associated type. We do need to make sure we use the same type, within the type that conforms to the protocol, wherever the associated type was used. Now let's see how we would use a generic type when creating a type that conforms to the `MyProtocol` protocol:

```
struct MyGenericType<T>: MyProtocol {
    var items: [T] = []
    mutating func add(item: T) {
        items.append(item)
    }
}
```

This code should look very familiar, as it is very similar to how we created a generic type. The T placeholder is used wherever the associated type is used in the protocol and when we create an instance of the MyGenericType type we will need to define what type to use.

Now let's see how we would use generics in a protocol-oriented design.

Generics in a protocol-oriented design

Now that we have seen how to use generics, let's see how we can use them in a protocol-oriented design. In a previous example in this chapter, we created a generic List type; however, we can greatly improve on this design and to do this we can look at how lists are used in the Java language.

When I was a Java developer, I used list types extensively. Java defines the List as an interface. An interface is very similar to the protocol in Swift and there are several types that conform to the List interface in Java. Let's see how we could design the list types in Swift using a protocol-oriented design. We will include only a small subset of the actual requirements for a list type so we can focus on the design rather than all of the requirements.

With a protocol-oriented design, we always start with the protocol. The following code shows the List protocol:

```
protocol List {
    associatedtype T
    mutating func add(item: T)
    func length() -> Int
    func get(index: Int) -> T?
}
```

We start the List protocol by defining the associated type T. This associated type will be the type of data stored in the list. We use the T type as the parameter for the add(item:) method and the return type for the get(index:) method. The add(item:) method will be used to add an item to the list, while the get(index:) method will be used to get the item at the specified index of the list. The length() method will return the number of items in the list.

From previous examples in this book, we may think that we would create a protocol extension for the `List` protocol; however, we want to keep our `List` protocol as generic as possible so we can use it for any type of list. We will see how this works as we go through the list examples. Let's start our examples with a really simple `ArrayList` type that will use an array as the backend storage mechanism. This example will show how we can create a type that conforms to the `List` protocol. Here is the code for the `ArrayList` type:

```
struct ArrayList<T>: List {
    private var items: [T] = []
    mutating func add(item: T) {
        items.append(item)
    }
    func length() -> Int {
        return items.count
    }
    func get(index: Int) -> T? {
        return items[index]
    }
}
```

While this type simply uses the interface provided by the Swift array type to provide the necessary functionality, it does hide the implementation details of the array and controls access to it. This is the proxy design pattern where we use one type to hide the implementation details of another type to control access to it.

We will create an instance of the `ArrayList` type and add items, as shown in the following code:

```
var arrayList = ArrayList<Int>()
arrayList.add(item: 1)
arrayList.add(item: 2)
arrayList.add(item: 3)
```

This code will create an instance of the `ArrayList` type that contains integers. We then add three integers to the `arrayList` instance. We can now use the `length()` method to get the number of items in the array list. We can also use the `get(index:)` method to get the item stored at a certain index. The following code shows this:

```
print("arrayList length: \(arrayList.length())")
print(arrayList.get(index: 1))
```

If we ran this code, we would see the following output:

```
arrayList length: 3
Optional(2)
```

This shows that we have three items in our list and the item at index one is an optional value that contains 2. There are two advantages to using a design such as this. The first is that we are hiding the implementation details of our backend storage. This allows us to change the storage type from an array to any other storage mechanism we may need in the future because we are using the interface provided by the List protocol to access the backend storage mechanism.

The second advantage we have with this design is we can access the instance of any type that conforms to the List protocol using the same interface. As an example, we may want to create a ShoppingCart type that conforms to the List protocol that persists the items in an SQLite database and use the same interface as we did with the ArrayList type.

Let's see how we could create a type that conforms to the List protocol that does not store the items in a Swift array. For this, we will create a type that will store the items in a linked list, but will still conform to the List protocol. If you are not familiar with linked lists, we explained how they worked in Chapter 2, *Our Type Choices*.

We will need to start off by creating a LinkedListNode type that will be used to store each value in our list. This will be a generic type so it will be able to store an instance of any type. The following code shows the LinkedListNode type:

```
class LinkedListNode<T> {
    var value: T
    var next: LinkedListNode?
    init(value: T) {
        self.value = value
    }
}
```

We will be creating a singly linked list so we will only need to store a reference to the next node in the list. The next property will contain this reference to the next node. We also have a generic property named value that will contain the value for the node. The initializer for this type requires us to provide the value for the node when we create a new instance.

Now let's create the LinkedList type that will conform to the List protocol. This type will be a generic type and will use the LinkedListNode type to store the values of the list. We will start off by defining the LinkedList type and specify that it conforms to the List protocol. We will also create two properties that will keep track of the first item in the list (named head) and the last item in the list (named tail):

```
class LinkedList<T>: List {

    var head: LinkedListNode<T>?
```

```
        var tail: LinkedListNode<T>?
    }
```

Now let's add the three required methods required by the `List` protocol. The first one we will add is the `add(item:)` method, which will add a node to the linked list:

```
func add(item: T) {
    let newItem = LinkedListNode(value: item)
    if let lastNode = tail {
        lastNode.next = newItem
        tail = newItem
    } else {
        head = newItem
        tail = newItem
    }
}
```

In this method, we create a new instance of the `LinkedListNode` type, named `newItem`, using the `item` parameter. We then check to see if the `tail` property contains a non-nil value and if so we add the new instance of the `LinkedListNode` type to the end of the list. We do this by pointing the `next` property of the last node to the new `LinkedListNode` instance and then set the last node to the new `LinkedListNode` instance.

If the `tail` property is nil, we create a new linked list by setting both the `head` and `tail` properties to the new `LinkedListNode` instance. Now let's create the `length()` method:

```
func length() -> Int {
    if var node = head {
        var count = 1
        while case let next? = node.next {
            node = next
            count += 1
        }
        return count
    } else {
        return 0
    }
}
```

To calculate the length of the linked list, we step through each node in the list until the `next` property of the node equals nil, which signifies that the node is the last node in the list.

Finally, let's create the `get(index:)` method for our `LinkedList` type:

```
func get(index: Int) -> T? {
    guard index >= 0 else {
        return nil
```

```
    }
    guard head != nil else {
        return nil
    }
    var node = head
    var i = index
    while (i > 0) {
        i -= 1
        if let newNode = node?.next {
            node = newNode
        } else {
            return nil
        }
    }
    return node?.value
}
```

We begin this method by verifying that the index parameter is greater than or equal to 0 and that the head property is not nil. If we pass both of these checks, the method will step through the linked list until we reach the end of the list or until we reach the node at the index we are looking for. If we reach the end of the list, we return nil indicating that we do not have a node at that index; otherwise we return the value of the node at the specified index.

There are two keys to this design that make it so powerful. The first key is we can create any list type that we need and if it conforms to the List protocol, we can use the interface provided by that protocol to interact with it. This allows us to create list types that have various backend storage mechanisms, but still use the same interface.

The second key and what makes designing our types with generics so powerful, is our list types can contain instances of any type. Let's see these two keys in action. We will start off by creating instances of both the ArrayList and LinkedList types and adding items to each:

```
var arrayList = ArrayList<Int>()
arrayList.add(item: 1)
arrayList.add(item: 2)
arrayList.add(item: 3)
print("ArrayList Length: \(arrayList.length())")
print("ArrayList item at index 1: \(arrayList.get(index: 1))")
var linkedList = LinkedList<Int>()
linkedList.add(item: 1)
linkedList.add(item: 2)
linkedList.add(item: 3)
print("LinkedList Length: \(linkedList.length())")
print("LinkedList item at index 1: \(linkedList.get(index: 1))")
```

If we run this code, we will see that both lists have a length of three and the value for index one is an optional value that is two.

Rather than storing integer values we could very easily store string values as follows:

```
let list = LinkedList<String>()
list.add(item: "item 1")
list.add(item: "item 2")
list.add(item: "item 3")
list.add(item: "item 4")
print(list.length())
print(list.get(index: 3))
```

Having the ability to store any type within our list types will allow our list types to not only work with the types we need today, but also any types we will be creating in the future. This is a very important consideration when we are designing our applications.

Summary

Generics in Swift are extremely powerful. With protocols, we are able to use a common interface to interact with various types that conform to the protocol. Also, when we use generics we are able to create generic types that can accept instances of any type. When we combine protocols and generics, as we saw with the List types in this chapter, we are able to create very powerful libraries that do not only meet our present needs, but also our future needs.

7
Adopting Design Patterns in Swift

While the first publication of the Gang of Four's *Design Patterns: Elements of Reusable Object-Oriented Software* was released in October of 1994, I have only been paying attention to design patterns for nine or ten years. Like most experienced developers, when I first started reading about design patterns, I recognized a lot of the patterns because I had already been using them without realizing what they were. I would have to say that in the past nine or ten years since I first read about design patterns, I have not written a serious application without using at least one of the Gang of Four's design patterns. I will tell you that I am definitely not a design pattern zealot, and if I get into a conversation about design patterns, there are usually only a couple of them that I can name without having to look them up. But one thing that I do remember is the concepts behind the major patterns and the problems they are designed to solve. This way, when I encounter one of these problems, I can look up the appropriate pattern and apply it. So, remember, as you go through this chapter, to take the time to understand the major concepts behind the design patterns rather than trying to memorize the patterns themselves.

In this chapter, you will learn about the following topics:

- What design patterns are
- What types of patterns make up the creational, structural, and behavioral categories of design patterns
- How to implement the builder, factory method, and singleton creational patterns in Swift
- How to implement the bridge, facade, and proxy structural patterns in Swift
- How to implement the strategy, command, and observer behavioral patterns in Swift

What are design patterns?

Every experienced developer has a set of informal strategies that shape how they design and write applications. These strategies are shaped by their past experiences and the obstacles that they have had to overcome in previous projects. While these developers might swear by their own strategies, it does not mean that their strategies have been fully vetted. The use of these strategies can also introduce inconsistent implementations between different projects and developers.

While the concept of design patterns dates back to the mid 80's, they did not gain popularity until the Gang of Four released their *Design Patterns: Elements of Reusable Object-Oriented Software* book, published in 1994. The book's authors, *Erich Gamma*, *Richard Helm*, *Ralph Johnson*, and *John Vlissides* (also known as the Gang of Four), discuss the pitfalls of object-oriented programming and describe 23 classic software design patterns. These 23 patterns are broken up into three categories: creational, structural, and behavioral.

A design pattern identifies a common software development problem and provides a strategy to deal with it. These strategies have been proven, over the years, to be an effective solution for the problems they are intended to solve. Using these patterns can greatly speed up the development process because they provide solutions that have already been proven to solve several common software development problems.

Another advantage that we get when we use design patterns is consistent code that is easy to maintain because, months or years from now, when we look at our code, we will recognize the patterns and understand what the code does. If we properly document our code and document the design pattern we are implementing, it will also help other developers understand what our code is doing.

The two main philosophies behind design patterns are code reuse and flexibility. As a software architect, it is essential that we build reusability and flexibility into our code. This allows us to easily maintain our code in the future and also makes it easier for our applications to expand to meet future requirements because we all know how quickly the requirements change.

While there is a lot to like about design patterns, and they are extremely beneficial for developers and architects, they are not the solution for world hunger that some developers make them out to be. At some time in your development career, you will probably meet a developer or an architect who thinks that design patterns are immutable laws. These developers usually try to force the use of design patterns even when they are not necessary. A good rule of thumb is to make sure that you have a problem that needs to be fixed before you try to fix it.

Design patterns are starting points for avoiding and solving common programming problems. We can think of each design pattern as a recipe for a food dish. Just like a good recipe, we can tinker and adjust it to meet our particular tastes. But we usually do not want to stray too far from the original recipe because we may mess it up.

There are also times when we do not have a recipe for a certain dish that we want to make just like there are times when there isn't a design pattern to solve the problem we face. In cases such as this, we can use our knowledge of design patterns and their underlying philosophy to come up with an effective solution for our problem.

Design patterns are split into three categories. They are as follows:

- **Creational patterns**: Creational patterns support the creation of objects
- **Structural patterns**: Structural patterns concern types and object compositions
- **Behavioral patterns**: Behavioral patterns communication between types

While the Gang of Four defined over 20 design patterns, we are only going to look at examples of some of the more popular patterns in this chapter. Let's start off by looking at creational patterns.

Design patterns were originally defined for object-oriented programming. In this chapter, we will focus on implementing the patterns in a more protocol-oriented way. Therefore, the examples in this chapter may look a little different from examples in other design pattern books, but the underlying philosophy of the solutions will be the same.

Creational patterns

Creational patterns are design patterns that deal with how an object is created. There are two basic ideas behind creational patterns. The first is encapsulating the knowledge of which concrete types should be created and the second is hiding how instances of these types are created.

There are five well-known patterns that are a part of the creational pattern category. They are as follows:

- **Abstract factory pattern**: This provides an interface for creating related objects without specifying the concrete type
- **Builder pattern**: This separates the construction of a complex object from its representation, so the same process can be used to create similar types

- **Factory method pattern**: This creates objects without exposing the underlying logic of how the object (or which type of object) is created
- **Prototype pattern**: This creates an object by cloning an existing one
- **Singleton pattern**: This allows one (and only one) instance of a class for the lifetime of an application

In this chapter, we are going to show examples of how to implement the builder, factory method, and singleton patterns in Swift. Let's start off by looking at one of the most controversial and possibly overused design patterns, the singleton pattern.

The singleton design pattern

The use of the singleton pattern is a fairly controversial subject among certain corners of the development community. One of the main reasons for this is that the singleton pattern is probably the most overused and misused pattern. Another reason this pattern is controversial is that the singleton pattern introduces a global state into an application, which provides the ability to change the object at any point within the application. The singleton pattern can also introduce hidden dependencies and tight compiling. My personal opinion is that if the singleton pattern is used correctly, there is nothing wrong with using it. However, we do need to be careful not to misuse it.

The singleton pattern restricts the instantiation of a class to a single instance for the lifetime of an application. This pattern is very effective when we need exactly one instance to coordinate actions within our application. An example of a good use of a singleton is if our application communicates with a remote device over Bluetooth and we also want to maintain that connection throughout our application. Some would say that we could pass the instance of the connection class from one page to the next, which is essentially what a singleton is. In my opinion, the singleton pattern, in this instance, is a much cleaner solution, because with the singleton pattern, any page that needs the connection can get it without forcing every page to maintain the instance. This also allows us to maintain the connection without having to reconnect each time we go to another page.

Understanding the problem

The problem the singleton pattern is designed to address is when we need one and only one instance of a type for the lifetime of our application. The singleton pattern is usually used when we need centralized management of an internal or external resource, and a single global point of access. Another popular use of the singleton pattern is when we want to consolidate a set of related activities, needed throughout our application, that do not maintain a state, in one place.

In Chapter 5, *Let's Extend Some Types*, we used the singleton pattern for our text validation types because we wanted to create a single instance of the types that could then be used by all the components of the application without requiring us to create new instances of the types. These text validation types did not have a state that could be changed. They only had methods that performed the validation on the text and constants that defined how to validate the text. While some may disagree with me, I believe types such as these are excellent candidates for the singleton pattern because there is no reason to create multiple instances of these types.

Understanding the solution

There are several ways to implement the singleton pattern in Swift. The way that is presented here uses class constants that were introduced in version 1.2 of Swift. With this method, a single instance of the class is created the first time we access the class constant. We will then use the class constant to gain access to this instance throughout the lifetime of our application. We will also create a private initializer that will prevent external code from creating additional instances of the class.

 Note that we use the word class in this description and not type. The reason for this is that the singleton pattern can only be implemented with reference types.

Implementing the singleton pattern

Let's look at how we implement the singleton pattern with Swift. The following code example shows how to create a singleton class:

```
class MySingleton {
    static let sharedInstance = MySingleton()
    var number = 0
    private init() {}

}
```

We can see that within the `MySingleton` class, we created a static constant named `sharedInstance` that contains an instance of the `MySingleton` class. A static constant can be called without having to instantiate the class. Since we declared the `sharedInstance` constant static, only one instance will exist throughout the lifecycle of the application, thereby creating the singleton pattern.

We also created the private initiator that will restrict other code from creating another instance of the `MySingleton` class.

Now, let's see how this pattern works. The `MySingleton` pattern has another property named `number`, which is of the `Int` type. We will monitor how this property changes as we use the `sharedInstance` property to create multiple variables of the `MySingleton` type, as shown in the following code:

```
var singleA = MySingleton.sharedInstance
var singleB = MySingleton.sharedInstance
var singleC = MySingleton.sharedInstance

singleB.number = 2

print(singleA.number)
print(singleB.number)
print(singleC.number)

singleC.number = 3

print(singleA.number)
print(singleB.number)
print(singleC.number)
```

In this example, we used the `sharedInstance` property to create three variables of the `MySingleton` type. We initially set the `number` property of the second `MySingleton` variable (`singleB`) to the number 2. When we printed out the value of the `number` property for `singleA`, `singleB`, and `singleC`, we saw that the `number` property for all three equals 2. We then changed the value of the `number` property of the third `MySingleton` variable (`singleC`) to the number 3. When we printed out the value of the `number` property again, we saw that all three now have the value of 3. Therefore, when we change the value of the `number` property in any of the instances, the values of all three change because each variable is pointed to the same instance.

In this example, we implemented the singleton pattern using a reference (class) type because we wanted to ensure that only one instance of the type existed throughout our application. If we implemented this pattern with a value type, such as a structure or an enumeration, we would run the risk of there being multiple instances of our type. If you recall, each time we pass an instance of a value type, we are actually passing a copy of that instance, which means that if we implemented the singleton pattern with a value type, each time we called the `sharedInstance` property, we would receive a new copy, which would effectively break the singleton pattern.

The singleton pattern can be very useful when we need to maintain the state of an object throughout our application; however, be careful not to overuse it. The singleton pattern should not be used unless there is a specific requirement (**requirement** is the keyword here) for having one, and only one, instance of our class throughout the lifecycle of our application. If we are using the singleton pattern simply for convenience, then we are probably misusing it.

Keep in mind that while Apple recommends that we prefer value types to reference types, there are still plenty of examples, such as the singleton pattern, where we need to use reference types. When we continuously tell ourselves to prefer value types to reference types, it can be very easy to forget that there are times where a reference type is needed. Don't forget to use reference types with this pattern.

Now, let's look at the builder design pattern.

The builder design pattern

The builder pattern helps us with the creation of complex objects and enforces the process of how these objects are created. With this pattern, we generally separate the creation logic from the complex type and put it in another type. This allows us to use the same construction process to create different representations of the type.

Understanding the problem

The problem that the builder problem is designed to address is when an instance of a type requires a large number of configurable values. We could set the configuration options when we create instances of the class, but that can cause issues if the options are not set correctly or we do not know the proper values for all of the options. Another issue is the amount of code that may be needed to set all of the configurable options each time we create an instance of our types.

Understanding the solution

The builder pattern solves this problem by introducing an intermediary known as a **builder** type. This builder type contains most, if not all, of the information necessary to create an instance of the original complex type.

There are two methods that we can use to implement the builder pattern. The first method is to have multiple builder types where each of the builder types contains the information to configure the original complex type in a specific way. The second method implements the builder pattern with a single builder type that sets all of the configurable options to a default value and then we would change the values as needed.

In this section, we will look at both ways to use the builder pattern because it is important to understand how each works.

Implementing the builder pattern

Before we show how we would use the builder pattern, let's look at how to create a complex structure without the builder pattern and the problem we run into.

The following code creates a structure named `BurgerOld` and does not use the builder pattern:

```
struct BurgerOld {
    var name: String
    var patties: Int
    var bacon: Bool
    var cheese: Bool
    var pickles: Bool
    var ketchup: Bool
    var mustard: Bool
    var lettuce: Bool
    var tomato: Bool
init(name: String, patties: Int, bacon: Bool, cheese: Bool, pickles:
Bool,ketchup: Bool,mustard: Bool,lettuce: Bool,tomato: Bool) {
        self.name = name
        self.patties = patties
        self.bacon = bacon
        self.cheese = cheese
        self.pickles = pickles
        self.ketchup = ketchup
        self.mustard = mustard
        self.lettuce = lettuce
        self.tomato = tomato
    }
}
```

In the `BurgerOld` structure, we have several properties that define which condiments are on the burger and also the name of the burger. Since we need to know which items are on the burgers, and which items aren't, when we create an instance of the `BurgerOld` structure, the initializer requires us to define each item. This can lead to some complex initializations throughout our application, not to mention that if we had more than one standard burger (bacon cheeseburger, cheeseburger, hamburger, and so on), we would need to make sure that each is defined correctly. Let's see how to create instances of the `BurgerOld` class:

```
// Create Hamburger
var burgerOld = BurgerOld(name: "Hamburger", patties: 1, bacon:   false,
cheese: false, pickles: false, ketchup: false, mustard:    false, lettuce:
false, tomato: false)

// Create Cheeseburger
var burgerOld = BurgerOld(name: "Cheeseburger", patties: 1, bacon:   false,
cheese: false, pickles: false, ketchup: false, mustard:    false, lettuce:
false, tomato: false)
```

As we can see, creating instances of the `BurgerOld` type requires a lot of code. Now, let's look at a better way to do this. In this example, we will show how to use multiple builder types where each type will define the condiments that are on a particular burger. We will begin by creating a `BurgerBuilder` protocol that will have the following code in it:

```
protocol BurgerBuilder {
    var name: String {get}
    var patties: Int {get}
    var bacon: Bool {get}
    var cheese: Bool {get}
    var pickles: Bool {get}
    var ketchup: Bool {get}
    var mustard: Bool {get}
    var lettuce: Bool {get}
    var tomato: Bool {get}
}
```

This protocol simply defines the nine properties that will be required for any type that implements this protocol. Now, let's create two structures that implement this protocol, the `HamburgerBuilder` and the `CheeseBurgerBuilder` structures:

```
struct HamBurgerBuilder: BurgerBuilder {
    let name = "Burger"
    let patties = 1
    let bacon = false
    let cheese = false
    let pickles = true
```

```
        let ketchup = true
        let mustard = true
        let lettuce = false
        let tomato = false
    }

    struct CheeseBurgerBuilder: BurgerBuilder {
        let name = "CheeseBurger"
        let patties = 1
        let bacon = false
        let cheese = true
        let pickles = true
        let ketchup = true
        let mustard = true
        let lettuce = false
        let tomato = false
    }
```

In both the `HamburgerBuilder` and the `CheeseBurgerBuilder` structures, all we are doing is defining the values for each of the required properties. In more complex types, we might need to initialize additional resources.

Now, let's look at our `Burger` structure, which will use instances of the `BurgerBuilder` protocol to create instances of itself. The following code shows this new `Burger` type:

```
    structure Burger {
        var name: String
        var patties: Int
        var bacon: Bool
        var cheese: Bool
        var pickles: Bool
        var ketchup: Bool
        var mustard: Bool
        var lettuce: Bool
        var tomato: Bool

        init(builder: BurgerBuilder) {
            self.name = builder.name
            self.patties = builder.patties
            self.bacon = builder.bacon
            self.cheese = builder.cheese
            self.pickles = builder.pickles
            self.ketchup = builder.ketchup
            self.mustard = builder.mustard
            self.lettuce = builder.lettuce
            self.tomato = builder.tomato
        }
```

```
func showBurger() {
        print("Name:      \(name)")
        print("Patties: \(patties)")
        print("Bacon:    \(bacon)")
        print("Cheese:   \(cheese)")
        print("Pickles: \(pickles)")
        print("Ketchup: \(ketchup)")
        print("Mustard: \(mustard)")
        print("Lettuce: \(lettuce)")
        print("Tomato:   \(tomato)")
    }
}
```

The difference between this `Burger` structure and the `BurgerOld` structure shown earlier is the initializer. In the previous `BurgerOld` structure, the initializer took nine arguments; one for each constant defined in the structure. In the new `Burger` structure, the initializer takes one argument, which is an instance of a type that conforms to the `BurgerBuilder` protocol. This new initializer allows us to create instances of the `Burger` class as follows:

```
// Create Hamburger
var myBurger = Burger(builder: HamBurgerBuilder())
myBurger.showBurger()
// Create Cheeseburger with tomatos
var myCheeseBurgerBuilder = CheeseBurgerBuilder()
var myCheeseBurger = Burger(builder: myCheeseBurgerBuilder)
// Lets hold the tomatos
myCheeseBurger.tomato = false
myCheeseBurger.showBurger()
```

If we compare how we create instances of the new `Burger` structure to the earlier `BurgerOld` structure, we can see that it is much easier to create instances of the `Burger` structure. We also know that we are correctly setting the property values for each type of burger because the values are set directly in the builder classes.

As we mentioned earlier, there is a second method that we can use to implement the builder pattern. Rather than having multiple builder types, we can have a single builder type that sets all of the configurable options to default values. We could then change the values as needed. I use this implementation method a lot when I am updating older code because it is easy to integrate it with preexisting code.

For this implementation, we will create a single `BurgerBuilder` structure. This `BurgerBuilder` structure will be used to create instances of the `BurgerOld` structure and will, by default, set all of the ingredients to their default values. The `BurgerBuilder` structure also gives us the ability to change what ingredients will go on the burger prior to creating instances of the `BurgerOld` structure. We create the `BurgerBuilder` structure as follows:

```
struct BurgerBuilder {
    var name = "Burger"
    var patties = 1
    var bacon = false
    var cheese = false
    var pickles = true
    var ketchup = true
    var mustard = true
    var lettuce = false
    var tomato = false
    mutating func setPatties(choice: Int) {self.patties = choice}
    mutating func setBacon(choice: Bool) {self.bacon = choice}
    mutating func setCheese(choice: Bool) {self.cheese = choice}
    mutating func setPickles(choice: Bool) {self.pickles = choice}
    mutating func setKetchup(choice: Bool) {self.ketchup = choice}
    mutating func setMustard(choice: Bool) {self.mustard = choice}
    mutating func setLettuce(choice: Bool) {self.lettuce = choice}
    mutating func setTomato(choice: Bool) {self.tomato = choice}
    func buildBurgerOld(name: String) -> BurgerOld {
        return BurgerOld(name: name, patties: self.patties,
            bacon: self.bacon, cheese: self.cheese,
            pickles: self.pickles, ketchup: self.ketchup,
            mustard: self.mustard, lettuce: self.lettuce,
            tomato: self.tomato)
    }
}
```

In the `BurgerBuilder` structure, we define our nine properties (ingredients) for our burger and then create a setter method for each of the properties except for the `name` property. We also create one method named `buildBurgerOld()` that will create an instance of the `BurgerOld` structure based on the values of the properties for the `BurgerBuilder` instance. We use the `BurgerBuilder` structure as follows:

```
var burgerBuilder = BurgerBuilder()
burgerBuilder.setCheese(choice: true)
burgerBuilder.setBacon(choice: true)
var jonBurger = burgerBuilder.buildBurgerOld(name: "Jon's Burger")
```

In this example, we create an instance of the `BurgerBuilder` structure. We then use the `setCheese()` and `setBacon()` methods to add cheese and bacon to our burger. Finally, we call the `buildBurgerOld()` method to create the instance of the `Burger` structure.

As we can see, both methods that were used to implement the builder pattern greatly simplify the creation of our complex type. Both methods also ensured that our instances were properly configured with default values. If you find yourself creating instances of types with very long and complex initialization commands, I would recommend that you look at the builder pattern to see if you can use it to simplify the initialization.

For our last example of a creational pattern, we will look at the factory method pattern.

The factory method pattern

The factory method pattern uses methods to create instances of objects without specifying the exact type that will be created. These methods are called **factory methods**. This allows us to pick the type to create at runtime.

I find that the factory pattern is one of the patterns that I use a lot. It is also one of the patterns that developers tend to recognize when they first start reading about design patterns because they have used it in previous projects.

Understanding the problem

The problem that the factory pattern is designed to solve is when there are multiple types that conform to a single protocol and we need to select the appropriate type to instantiate at runtime.

Understanding the solution

The factory method pattern encapsulates the logic used to select which type to instantiate within a single method. This method exposes only the protocol (or base class) to the code that calls it and does not reveal the details of how a particular type was selected.

Implementing the factory method pattern

To demonstrate how we would use the factory method pattern, we will use the text validation types that we created at the end of Chapter 5, *Let's Extend Some Types*. In this example, we will create a function that will determine which text validation type to use based on the parameters passed into the factory method by the code that called it. As a refresher, the code for the TextValidationProtocol protocol and the TextValidationProtocol protocol extension are shown in the following code:

```
protocol TextValidationProtocol {
    var regExFindMatchString: String {get}
    var validationMessage: String {get}
}

extension TextValidationProtocol {
    var regExMatchingString: String { get {
        return regExFindMatchString + "$"
        }
    }
    func validateString(str: String) -> Bool {
        if let _ =  str.range(of: regExMatchingString, options:
            .regularExpression) {
            return true
        } else {
            return false
        }
    }
    func getMatchingString(str: String) -> String? {
        if let newMatch =  str.range(of: regExFindMatchString,
            options: .regularExpression) {
            return str.substring(with: newMatch)
        } else {
            return nil
        }
    }
}
```

Within the TextValidationProtocol protocol, we define two properties named regExFindMatchString and validationMessage. Within the protocol extension, we implement one computed property named regExMatchingString and two methods named validateString() and getMatchingString().

Now let's create three types that conform to the `TextValidationProtocol` protocol. These three types will be named `AlphaValidation`, `NumericValidation`, and `AlphaNumericValidation`:

```
class AlphaValidation: TextValidationProtocol {
    static let sharedInstance = AlphaValidation()
    private init(){}
    let regExFindMatchString = "^[a-zA-Z]{0,10}"
    let validationMessage = "Can only contain Alpha characters"
}

class AlphaNumericValidation: TextValidationProtocol {
    static let sharedInstance = AlphaNumericValidation()
    private init(){}
    let regExFindMatchString = "^[a-zA-Z0-9]{0,10}"
    let validationMessage = "Can only contain Alpha Numeric
        characters"
}

class NumericValidation: TextValidationProtocol {
    static let sharedInstance = NumericValidation()
    private init(){}
    let regExFindMatchString = "^[0-9]{0,10}"
    let validationMessage = "Display Name can contain a maximum of
        15 Alphanumeric Characters"
}
```

The `AlphaValidation` class can be used to validate strings to ensure that they contain a maximum of 10 alpha characters. The `NumericValidation` class can be used to validate strings to ensure that they contain a maximum of 10 numeric characters. Finally, the `AlphaNumericValidation` class can be used to validate strings to ensure that they contain a maximum of 10 alpha and/or numeric characters.

To use these validation classes, we need a way to determine which class to use based on the string that we are validating. The factory method pattern can help us with this determination. We could implement this pattern as follows:

```
func getValidator(alphaCharacters: Bool, numericCharacters: Bool) ->
TextValidationProtocol? {
    if alphaCharacters && numericCharacters {
        return AlphaNumericValidation.sharedInstance
    } else if alphaCharacters && !numericCharacters {
        return AlphaValidation.sharedInstance
    } else if !alphaCharacters && numericCharacters {
        return NumericValidation.sharedInstance
    } else {
```

```
            return nil
        }
    }
```

The `getValidator()` method accepts two parameters both of the Boolean type named `alphaCharacters` and `numericCharacters`. These parameters define the type of validation we wish to do and we then return a type that conforms to the `TextValidationProtocol` protocol based on the values in the parameters.

One of the biggest advantages that we get with this pattern is that all of the logic on how the text validation types are selected is encapsulated in this one function. This means that if we need to change the logic or change which type to use, the only code we need to change is the code within this function rather than having to refactor our entire code base. As an example, if we wish to replace the `AlphaValidation` class with a new `AlphaSpacesValidation` class, the only code that needs to change is within this function.

We can now use the `getValidator()` method, as shown in the following code:

```
var str = "abc123"
var validator1 = getValidator(alphaCharacters: true,
numericCharacters: false)
print("String validated: \(validator1?.validateString(str: str))")

var validator2 = getValidator(alphaCharacters: true,
numericCharacters: true)
print("String validated: \(validator2?.validateString(str: str))")
```

In this code, the `validator1` variable contains an instance of the `AlphaValidation` type. When we call the `validateString()` method of this instance, it returns a false value because the `str` variable contains numeric values. The `validator2` variable contains an instance of the `AlphaNumericValidation` type. When we call the `validateString()` method of this instance, it returns `true` because the validation class looks for both alpha and numeric characters.

One of the key ideas behind creational patterns is that we take the logic about how and what to create out of our general code base and put it into specific classes or functions. Then, when we need to make changes to our code in the future, the logic is encapsulated in a single spot and can be easily changed, rather than having the logic spread throughout our code.

Now, let's look at structural design patterns.

Structural design patterns

Structural design patterns describe how types can be combined to form larger structures. These larger structures can generally be easier to work with and hide a lot of the complexity of the individual types. Most patterns in the structural pattern category involve connections between objects.

There are seven well-known patterns that are part of the structural design pattern type. These are as follows:

- **Adapter**: This allows types with incompatible interfaces to work together
- **Bridge**: This is used to separate the abstract elements of a type from the implementation, so the two can vary
- **Composite**: This allows us to treat a group of objects as a single object
- **Decorator**: This lets us add or override behavior in an existing method of an object
- **Facade**: This provides a simplified interface for a larger and more complex body of code
- **Flyweight**: This allows us to reduce the resources needed to create and use a large number of similar objects
- **Proxy**: This is a type acting as an interface for another class or classes

In this chapter, we are going to give examples of how to use bridge, facade, and proxy patterns in Swift. Let's start off by looking at the bridge pattern.

The bridge pattern

The bridge pattern decouples the abstraction from the implementation so that they can both vary independently. The bridge pattern can also be thought of as a two-layer abstraction.

Understanding the problem

The bridge pattern is designed to solve a couple of problems, but the one we are going to focus on here tends to arise over time as new requirements come in with new features. At some point, as these new requirements and features come in, we will need to change how the features interact. Usually, this will require us to refactor our code.

In object-oriented programming, this is known as an **exploding class hierarchy**, but it can also happen in protocol-oriented programming.

Understanding the solution

The bridge pattern solves this problem by taking the interacting features and separating the functionality that is specific to each feature from the functionality that is shared between them. A bridge type can then be created, which will encapsulate the shared functionality, bringing them together.

Implementing the bridge pattern

To demonstrate how we would use the bridge pattern, we will create two features. The first feature is a message feature that will store and prepare a message that we wish to send out. The second feature is the sender feature that will send the message through a specific channel such as e-mail or SMS messaging.

Let's start off by creating two protocols named `MessageProtocol` and `SenderProtocol`. The `MessageProtocol` protocol will define the requirements for types that are used to create messages. The `SenderProtocol` protocol will be used to define the requirements for types that are used to send the messages through the specific channels. The following code shows how we would define these two protocols:

```
protocol MessageProtocol {
    var messageString: String {get set}
    init(messageString: String)
    func prepareMessage()
}

protocol SenderProtocol {
    func sendMessage(message: MessageProtocol)
}
```

The `MessageProtocol` protocol defines one stored property named `messageString` of the `String` type. This property will contain the text of the message and cannot be nil. We also define one initiator and a method named `prepareMessage()`. The initiator will be used to set the `messageString` property and anything else required by the message type. The `prepareMessage()` method will be used to prepare the message prior to sending it. This method can be used to encrypt the message, add formatting, or do anything else to the message prior to sending it.

The `SenderProtocol` protocol defines one method named `sendMessage()`. This method will send the message through the channel defined by conforming types. In this function, we will need to ensure that the `prepareMessage()` method from the message type is called prior to sending the message.

Now let's see how we would define two types that conform to the `MessageProtocol` protocol:

```
class PlainTextMessage: MessageProtocol {
    var messageString: String
    required init(messageString: String) {
        self.messageString = messageString
    }
    func prepareMessage() {
        //  Nothing to do
    }
}

class DESEncryptedMessage: MessageProtocol {
    var messageString: String
    required init(messageString: String) {
        self.messageString = messageString
    }
    func prepareMessage() {
    // Encrypt message here
        self.messageString = "DES: " + self.messageString
    }
}
```

Each of these types contains the required functionality to conform to the `MessageProtocol` protocol. The only real difference between these types is in the `prepareMessage()` methods. In the `PlainTextMessage` class, the `prepareMessage()` method is empty because we do not need to do anything to the message prior to sending it. The `prepareMessage()` method of the `DESEncryptionMessage` class would normally contain the logic to encrypt the message, but for our example we will just prepend a `DES` tag to the beginning of the message, letting us know that this method was called.

Now let's create two types that will conform to the `SenderProtocol` protocol. These types would typically handle sending the message through a specific channel; however, in our example we will simply print a message to the console:

```
class EmailSender: SenderProtocol {
    func sendMessage(message: MessageProtocol) {
        print("Sending through E-Mail:")
        print(" \(message.messageString)")
    }
}

class SMSSender: SenderProtocol {
    func sendMessage(message: MessageProtocol) {
        print("Sending through SMS:")
```

```
            print(" \(message.messageString)")
        }
    }
```

Both the `EmailSender` and the `SMSSender` types conform to the `SenderProtocol` protocol by implementing the `sendMessage()` function.

We could now use these two features, as shown in the following code:

```
var myMessage = PlainTextMessage(messageString: "Plain Text Message")
message.prepareMessage()
var sender = SMSSender()
sender.sendMessage(message: message)
```

This would work great and we could add code similar to this anywhere we needed to create and send a message. Let's say that one day in the near future, we get a requirement to add new functionality that would verify the message prior to sending it to make sure it meets the requirements of the channel we are sending the message through. To do this, we would start off by changing the `SenderProtocol` protocol to add the verify functionality. The new sender protocol would look as follows:

```
protocol SenderProtocol {
    var message: MessageProtocol? {get set}
    func sendMessage()
    func verifyMessage()
}
```

To the `SenderProtocol` protocol, we added a method named `verifyMessage()` and also added a property named `message`. We also changed the definition of the `sendMessage()` method. The original `SenderProtocol` protocol was designed to simply send the message, but now we need to verify the message prior to calling the `sendMessage()` function; therefore, we couldn't simply pass the message to the sender as we did in the previous definition.

Now we will need to change the types that conform to the `SenderProtocol` protocol to make them conform to this new protocol. The following code shows how we would make these changes:

```
class EmailSender: SenderProtocol {
    var message: MessageProtocol?
    func sendMessage() {
        print("Sending through E-Mail:")
        print(" \(message!.messageString)")
    }
    func verifyMessage() {
        print("Verifying E-Mail message")
```

```
        }
    }

class SMSSender: SenderProtocol {
    var message: MessageProtocol?
    func sendMessage() {
        print("Sending through SMS:")
        print(" \(message!.messageString)")
    }
    func verifyMessage() {
        print("Verifying SMS message")
    }
}
```

With the changes that we made to the types that conform to the `SenderProtocol` protocol, we will need to change how our code uses these types. The following example shows how we would now use them:

```
var myMessage = PlainTextMessage(messageString: "Plain Text Message")
message.prepareMessage()
var sender = SMSSender()
sender.message = message
sender.verifyMessage()
sender.sendMessage()
```

These changes are not that hard to make; however, without the bridge pattern, we would need to refactor our entire code base and make the change everywhere that we are sending messages. The bridge pattern tells us that when we have two hierarchies that closely interact together such as this; we should put this interaction logic into a bridge type that will encapsulate the logic in one spot. This way, when we receive new requirements or enhancements, we can make the change in one spot, thereby limiting the refactoring that we are required to do. We could make a bridge type for our message and sender hierarchies, as shown in the following example:

```
struct MessageingBridge
static func sendMessage(message: MessageProtocol, sender: SenderProtocol)
    {
        var sender = sender
        message.prepareMessage()
        sender.message = message
        sender.verifyMessage()
        sender.sendMessage()
    }
}
```

Now the logic of how our messaging and sender hierarchies interact is encapsulated into the `MessagingBridge` structure. Therefore, when the logic needs to change, we make the change to this one structure rather than having to refactor our entire code base.

The bridge pattern is a very good pattern to remember and use. There have been (and still are) times that I have regretted not using the bridge pattern in my code because, as we all know, requirements change frequently and being able to make the changes in one spot rather than throughout the code base can save us a lot of time in the future.

Now, let's look at the next pattern in the structural category-the facade pattern.

The facade pattern

The facade pattern provides a simplified interface to a larger and more complex body of code. This allows us to make our libraries easier to use and understand by hiding some of the complexities. It also allows us to combine multiple API's into a single, easier to use API, which is what we will see in our example.

Understanding the problem

The facade pattern is often used when we have a complex system that has a large number of independent APIs that are designed to work together. Sometimes it is hard to tell where we should use the facade pattern during our initial application design. The reason for this is that we normally try to simplify our initial API design; however, over time and as requirements change and new features are added, our APIs become more and more complex, and then it becomes pretty evident where we should have used the facade pattern. A good rule to use is: if you have several APIs that are working closely together to perform a task, you should think about using the facade pattern.

Understanding the solution

The main idea of the facade pattern is to hide the complexity of our APIs behind a simple interface. This offers us several advantages, with the most obvious being that it simplifies how we interact with the APIs. It also promotes loose coupling, which allows our APIs to change, as requirements change, without the need to refactor all of the code that uses them.

Implementing the facade pattern

To demonstrate the facade pattern, we will create three APIs: `HotelBooking`, `FlightBooking`, and `RentalCarBooks`. These APIs will be used to search for and book hotels, flights, and rental cars for trips. While we could very easily call each of the APIs individually in our code, we are going to create a `TravelFacade` structure that will allow us to access the functionality of the APIs in single calls.

We will begin by defining the three APIs. Each of the APIs will need a data storage class that will store the information about the hotel, flight, or rental car. We will start off by implementing the hotel API:

```
struct Hotel {
    //Information about hotel room
}

struct HotelBooking {
    static func getHotelNameForDates(to: NSDate, from: NSDate) ->
      [Hotel]? {
        let hotels = [Hotel]()
        //logic to get hotels
        return hotels
    }

    static func bookHotel(hotel: Hotel) {
        // logic to reserve hotel room
    }
}
```

The hotel API consists of `Hotel` and `HotelBooking` structures. The `Hotel` structure will be used to store the information about a hotel room and the `HotelBooking` structure will be used to search for a hotel room and also to book the room for our trip. The flight and rental car APIs are very similar to the hotel API. The following code shows both of these APIs:

```
struct Flight {
    //Information about flights
}

struct FlightBooking {
    static func getFlightNameForDates(to: NSDate, from: NSDate) ->
      [Flight]? {
        let flights = [Flight]()
        //logic to get flights
        return flights
    }
}
```

```
        static func bookFlight(fight: Flight) {
            // logic to reserve flight
        }
    }


    struct RentalCar {
        //Information about rental cars
    }

    struct RentalCarBooking {
        static func getRentalCarNameForDates(to: NSDate, from: NSDate)
          -> [RentalCar]? {
            let cars = [RentalCar]()
            //logic to get flights
            return cars
        }

        static func bookRentalCar(rentalCar: RentalCar) {
            // logic to reserve rental car
        }
    }
```

In each of these APIs, we have a structure that is used to store information and a structure that is used to provide the search/booking functionality. In our initial design, it would be very easy to call these individual APIs within our application; however, as we all know, requirements tend to change, which causes our APIs to change over time. By using the facade pattern here, we are able to hide how we implement the APIs; therefore, if we need to change how the APIs work in the future, we will only need to update the facade type rather than refactoring all of our code. This makes our code easier to maintain and update in the future. Now let's look at how we will implement the facade pattern by creating a TravelFacade class:

```
    class TravelFacade {

        var hotels: [Hotel]?
        var flights: [Flight]?
        var cars: [RentalCar]?

        init(to: NSDate, from: NSDate) {
            hotels = HotelBooking.getHotelNameForDates(to: to, from: from)
            flights = FlightBooking.getFlightNameForDates(to: to, from:
                from)
            cars = RentalCarBooking.getRentalCarNameForDates(to: to, from:
                from)
        }
```

```
    func bookTrip(hotel: Hotel, flight: Flight, rentalCar:
      RentalCar) {
        HotelBooking.bookHotel(hotel: hotel)
        FlightBooking.bookFlight(flight: flight)
        RentalCarBooking.bookRentalCar(rentalCar: rentalCar)
    }
}
```

The `TravelFacade` class contains the functionality to search the three APIs and also book a hotel, flight, and rental car. We can now use the `TravelFacade` class to search for hotels, flights, and rental cars without having to directly access the individual APIs. We can also use the `TravelFacade` class to book our hotel, flights, and rental cars without having to access the individual APIs.

As we mentioned at the start of this chapter, it is not always obvious where we should use the facade pattern in our initial design. A good rule to follow is: if we have several APIs that are working together to perform a task, we should think about using the facade pattern.

Now, let's look at our last structural pattern, which is the proxy design pattern.

The proxy design pattern

In the proxy design pattern, there is one type acting as an interface for another type or API. This wrapper class, which is the proxy, can then add functionality to the object, make the object available over a network, or restrict access to the object.

Understanding the problem

We can use the proxy pattern to solve a number of problems, but I find that I mainly use this pattern to solve two problems.

The first problem that I use the proxy pattern to solve is when I want to create a layer of abstraction between a single API and my code. The API could be a local or remote API, but I usually use this pattern to put an abstraction layer between my code and a remote service. This will allow changes to the remote API without the need to refactor large portions of our code.

The second problem that I use the proxy pattern to solve is when I need to make changes to an API, but I do not have the code or there is already a dependency on the API elsewhere in the application.

Understanding the solution

To solve these problems, the proxy pattern tells us that we should create a type that will act as an interface for interacting with the other type or API. In our example, we will show how to use the proxy pattern to add functionality to an existing type.

Implementing the proxy pattern

In this section, we will demonstrate the proxy pattern by creating a house class that we can add multiple floor plans to, where each floor plan represents a different storey of the house. Let's begin by creating a FloorPlanProtocol protocol:

```swift
protocol FloorPlanProtocol {
    var bedRooms: Int {get set}
    var utilityRooms: Int {get set}
    var bathRooms: Int {get set}
    var kitchen: Int {get set}
    var livingRooms: Int {get set}
}
```

In the FloorPlanProtocol protocol, we define five properties that will represent the number of rooms contained in each floor plan. Now, let's create an implementation of the FloorPlanProtocol protocol named FloorPlan, which is as follows:

```swift
struct FloorPlan: FloorPlanProtocol {
    var bedRooms = 0
    var utilityRooms = 0
    var bathRooms = 0
    var kitchen = 0
    var livingRooms = 0
}
```

The FloorPlan class implements all five properties required from FloorPlanProtocol and assigns default values to them. Next, we will create the House class, which will represent a house:

```swift
class House {
    internal var stories = [FloorPlanProtocol]()
    func addStory(floorPlan: FloorPlanProtocol) {
        stories.append(floorPlan)
    }
}
```

Within our `House` class, we have an array of `FloorPlanProtocol` objects where each floor plan will represent one storey of the house. We also have one function named `addStory()`, which accepts an instance of a type that conforms to the `FloorPlanProtocol` protocol. This function will add the floor plan to the array of `FloorPlanProtocol` protocols.

If we think about the logic of this class, there is one problem that we might encounter. The problem is we are allowed to add as many floor plans as we want, which may lead to houses that are 60 or 70 stories high. This would be great if we were building skyscrapers, but we just want to build basic single-family houses. If we want to limit the number of floor plans without changing the `House` class (either we cannot change it or we simply do not want to), we can implement the proxy pattern. The following example shows how to implement the `HouseProxy` class, where we limit the number of floor plans we can add to the house, as follows:

```
class HouseProxy {
  var house = House()
   func addStory(floorPlan: FloorPlanProtocol) -> Bool {
     if house.stories.count < 3 {
       house.addStory(floorPlan: floorPlan)
       return true
     }
     else {
       return false
     }
   }
}
```

We begin the `HouseProxy` class by creating an instance of the `House` class. We then create a method named `addStory()` that lets us add a new floor plan to the house. In the `addStory()` method, we check to see if the number of stories in the house is fewer than three; if so, we add the floor plan to the house and return `true`. If the number of stories is equal to or greater than three, then we do not add the floor plan to the house and return `false`. Let's see how we would use this proxy:

```
var ourHouse = HouseProxy()

var basement = FloorPlan(bedRooms: 0, utilityRooms: 1, bathRooms:    1,
kitchen: 0, livingRooms: 1)
var firstStory = FloorPlan(bedRooms: 1, utilityRooms: 0,    bathRooms: 2,
kitchen: 1, livingRooms: 1)
var secondStory = FloorPlan(bedRooms: 2, utilityRooms: 0,    bathRooms: 1,
kitchen: 0, livingRooms: 1)
var additionalStory = FloorPlan(bedRooms: 1, utilityRooms: 0,    bathRooms:
1, kitchen: 1, livingRooms: 1)
```

```
print(ourHouse.addStory(floorPlan: basement))
print(ourHouse.addStory(floorPlan: firstStory))
print(ourHouse.addStory(floorPlan: secondStory))
print(ourHouse.addStory(floorPlan: additionalStory))
```

In our example code, we start off by creating an instance of the `HouseProxy` class named `ourHouse`. We then create four instances of the `FloorPlan` class, each with a different number of rooms. Finally, we attempt to add each of the floor plans to the `ourHouse` instance. If we then run the code, we will see that the first three instances of the `floorplan` class were added to the house successfully, but the last one wasn't because we are only allowed to add three floors.

The proxy pattern is very useful when we want to add some additional functionality or error checking to a type, but we do not want to change the actual type itself. We can also use it to add a layer of abstraction between a remote or local API.

Now, let's look at behavioral design patterns.

Behavioral design patterns

Behavioral design patterns explain how types interact with each other. These patterns describe how different instances of types send messages to each other to make things happen.

There are nine well-known patterns that are part of the behavioral design pattern type. They are as follows:

- **Chain of responsibility**: This is used to process a variety of requests, each of which may be delegated to a different handler.
- **Command**: This creates objects that can encapsulate actions or parameters so that they can be invoked later or by a different component.
- **Iterator**: This allows us to access the elements of an object sequentially without exposing the underlying structure.
- **Mediator**: This is used to reduce coupling between types that communicate with each other.
- **Memento**: This is used to capture the current state of an object and store it in a manner that can be restored later.
- **Observer**: This allows an object to publish changes to its state. Other objects can then subscribe so they can be notified of any changes.
- **State**: This is used to alter the behavior of an object when its internal state changes.

- **Strategy**: This allows one out of a family of algorithms to be chosen at runtime.
- **Visitor**: This is a way of separating an algorithm from an object structure.

In this section, we are going to give examples of how to use strategy, observer, and command patterns in Swift. Let's start off by looking at the command pattern.

The command design pattern

The command design pattern lets us define actions that we can execute later. This pattern generally encapsulates all the information needed to call or trigger the actions at a later time.

Understanding the problem

There are times in our applications when we need to separate the execution of a command from its invoker. Typically, this is when we have a type that needs to perform one of several actions; however, the choice of which action to use needs to be made at runtime.

Understanding the solution

The command pattern tells us that we should encapsulate the logic for the actions into a type that conforms to a command protocol. We can then provide instances of the command types for use by the invoker. The invoker will use the interface provided by the protocol to invoke the needed actions.

Implementing the command pattern

In this section, we will demonstrate how to use the command pattern by creating a `Light` type. In this type, we will define the `lightOnCommand` and `lightOffCommand` commands and will use the `turnOnLight()` and `turnOffLight()` methods to invoke these commands.

We will begin by creating a protocol named `Command` that all of our command types will conform to. Here is the `Command` protocol:

```
protocol Command {
  func execute()
}
```

This protocol contains one method named `execute`, which will be used to execute the command. Now, let's look at our command types that the `Light` type will use to turn the light on and off. They are as follows:

```swift
struct RockerSwitchLightOnCommand: Command {
  func execute() {
    print("Rocker Switch:  Turning Light On")
  }
}

struct RockerSwitchLightOffCommand: Command {
  func execute() {
    print("Rocker Switch:  Turning Light Off")
  }
}
struct PullSwitchLightOnCommand: Command {
  func execute() {
    print("Pull Switch:  Turning Light On")
  }
}

struct PullSwitchLightOffCommand: Command {
  func execute() {
    print("Pull Switch:  Turning Light Off")
  }
}
```

The `RockerSwitchLightOffCommand`, `RockerSwitchLightOnCommand`, `PullSwitchLightOnCommand`, and `PullSwitchLightOffCommand` commands all conform to the `Command` protocol by implementing the `execute()` method; therefore, we will be able to use them in our `Light` type. Now, let's look at how to implement the `Light` type:

```swift
class Light {
  var lightOnCommand: Command
  var lightOffCommand: Command
  init(lightOnCommand: Command, lightOffCommand: Command) {
    self.lightOnCommand = lightOnCommand
    self.lightOffCommand = lightOffCommand
  }
  func turnOnLight() {
    self.lightOnCommand.execute()
  }
  func turnOffLight() {
    self.lightOffCommand.execute()
  }
}
```

In the `Light` type, we start off by creating two variables named `lightOnCommand` and `lightOffCommand` that will contain instances of types that conform to the `Command` protocol. We then create an initiator that lets us set both of the commands when we initiate the type. Finally, we create the `turnOnLight()` and `turnOffLight()` methods that we will use to turn the light on and off. In these methods, we call the appropriate command to turn the light on or off.

We would then use the `Light` type as follows:

```
var on = PullSwitchLightOnCommand()
var off = PullSwitchLightOffCommand()
var light = Light(lightOnCommand: on, lightOffCommand: off)

light.turnOnLight()
light.turnOffLight()

light.lightOnCommand = RockerSwitchLightOnCommand()
light.turnOnLight()
```

In this example, we begin by creating an instance of the `PullSwitchLightOnCommand` type named `on` and an instance of the `PullSwitchLightOffCommand` type named `off`. We then create an instance of the `Light` type using the two commands that we just created and call the `turnOnLight()` and `turnOffLight()` methods of the `Light` instance to turn our light on and off. In the last two lines, we change the `lightOnCommand` method, which was originally set to an instance of the `PullSwitchLightOnCommand` class, to an instance of the `RockerSwitchLightOnCommand` type. The `Light` instance will now use the `RockerSwitchLightOnCommand` type whenever we turn the light on. This allows us to change the functionality of the `Light` type during runtime.

There are a number of benefits to using the command pattern. One of the main benefits is that we are able to set which command to invoke at runtime, which also lets us swap the commands out with different implementations that conform to the `Command` protocol as needed throughout the life of the application. Another advantage of the command pattern is that we encapsulate the details of the command implementations within the command types themselves rather than in the container type.

Now, let's look at the strategy pattern.

The strategy pattern

The strategy pattern is pretty similar to the command pattern in that they both allow us to decouple implementation details from our calling type and also allow us to switch the implementation out at runtime. The big difference is the strategy pattern is intended to encapsulate algorithms. By swapping out an algorithm, we are expecting the object to perform the same functionality, but in a different way. In the command pattern, when we swap out the commands, we are expecting the object to change the functionality of the object.

Understanding the problem

There are times in our applications when we need to change the backend algorithm that is used to perform an operation. Typically this is when we have a type that has several different algorithms that can be used to perform the same task; however, the choice of which algorithm to use needs to be made at runtime.

Understanding the solution

The strategy pattern tells us that we should encapsulate the algorithm in a type that conforms to a strategy protocol. We can then provide instances of the strategy types for use by the invoker. The invoker will use the interface provided by the protocol to invoke the algorithm.

Implementing the strategy pattern

In this section, we will demonstrate the strategy pattern by showing you how we could swap out compression strategies at runtime. Let's begin this example by creating a CompressionStrategy protocol that each one of our compression types will conform to. Let's take a look at the following code:

```
protocol CompressionStrategy {
  func compressFiles(filePaths: [String])
}
```

This protocol defines one method named `compressFiles()` that accepts a single parameter, which is an array of strings that contain the paths to the files we want to compress. We will now create two structures that conform to the `CompressionStrategy` protocol. These are the `ZipCompressionStrategy` and the `RarCompressionStrategy` structures, which are as follows:

```
struct ZipCompressionStrategy: CompressionStrategy {
  func compressFiles(filePaths: [String]) {
    print("Using Zip Compression")
  }
}

struct RarCompressionStrategy: CompressionStrategy {
  func compressFiles(filePaths: [String]) {
    print("Using RAR Compression")
  }
}
```

Both of these structures implement the `CompressionStrategy` protocol by having a method named `compressFiles()`, which accepts an array of strings. Within these methods, we simply print out the name of the compression that we are using. Normally we would implement the compression logic in these methods.

Now, let's look at our `CompressContent` class, which will be called to compress the files:

```
class CompressContent {
  var strategy: CompressionStrategy
  init(strategy: CompressionStrategy) {
    self.strategy = strategy
  }
  func compressFiles(filePaths: [String]) {
    self.strategy.compressFiles(filePaths: filePaths)
  }
}
```

In this class, we start off by defining a variable-named strategy that will contain an instance of a type that conforms to the `CompressStrategy` protocol. We then create an initiator that will be used to set the compression type when the class is initiated. Finally, we create a method named `compressFiles()` that accepts an array of strings that contain the paths to the list of files that we wish to compress. In this method, we compress the files using the compression strategy that is set in the strategy variable.

We will use the `CompressContent` class as follows:

```
var filePaths = ["file1.txt", "file2.txt"]
var zip = ZipCompressionStrategy()
var rar = RarCompressionStrategy()

var compress = CompressContent(strategy: zip)
compress.compressFiles(filePaths: filePaths)

compress.strategy = rar
compress.compressFiles(filePaths: filePaths)
```

We begin by creating an array of strings that contain the files we wish to compress. We also create an instance of both the `ZipCompressionStrategy` and the `RarCompressionStrategy` types. We then create an instance of the `CompressContent` class, setting the compression strategy to the `ZipCompressionStrategy` instance, and call the `compressFiles()` method, which will print the `Using zip compression` message to the console. We then set the compression strategy to the `RarCompressionStrategy` instance and call the `compressFiles()` method again, which will print the `Using rar compression` message to the console.

The strategy pattern is really good for setting the algorithms to use at runtime, which also lets us swap the algorithms out with different implementations as needed by the application. Another advantage of the strategy pattern is we encapsulate the details of the algorithm within the strategy types themselves and not in the main implementation type.

Now let's look at one last pattern, the observer pattern.

The observer pattern

The observer pattern is used to implement distributed event handling where an observer type is notified when an event occurs within another type. The observer pattern allows groups of objects to cooperate with one another with few dependencies between them. This pattern is so widely used that you have probably come across it many times if you have developed applications using any modern UI framework such as Cocoa or Cocoa Touch.

Understanding the problem

There are times where we need to perform an action in one or more parts of our code when some event happens in another part of our code. This is a very common requirement with most modern UI frameworks, where we wish to be notified when the user has had some interaction with our user interface.

Understanding the solution

With the observer pattern, the observer registers to be notified when an event happens. When the event is triggered, any instance that has registered for the event receives a notification that the event has occurred. In Swift, there are several ways that we can implement the observer pattern and in this section we will look at three of them. We are looking at multiple solutions for this pattern because each of these solutions helps us implement the observer pattern under specific circumstances. We will talk about when to use each one of these solutions as we talk about the solutions themselves.

Implementing the observer pattern

For the first solution, we will use the `NotificationCenter` class. The `NotificaitionCenter` class provides us with a mechanism to register for, post, and receive notifications. All Cocoa- and Cocoa Touch-based applications have a default notification center when they are running. There is no need to create our own instance of the `NotificationCenter` class.

When we use the notification center we need to provide a name for each notification. One thing we never want to do is to hard code the name in both the notifying type (the type that posts the notifications) and the receiving types (the types that receive the notifications). Instead we will want to define the name in a global constant and use it for both the notifying and the receiving types; therefore, we will begin this example by defining the name for our notification as follows:

```
let NCNAME = "Notification Name"
```

Now we will create the type that will post our notifications. In this example, our type will simply post a notification to the default notification center when we call a method named `post`:

```
class PostType {
    let nc = NotificationCenter.default
    func post() {
        nc.post(name: Notification.Name(rawValue: NCNAME), object: nil)
    }
}
```

Finally, we will create a type that will receive the notifications when they are posted to the notification center. This type will register a selector (in this example, a method named `receivedNotification()`) with the notification center that will be called when new notifications, identified by the name, are posted to the notification center:

```
class ObserverType {
    let nc = NotificationCenter.default
    init() {
        nc.addObserver(self, selector:
        #selector(receiveNotification(notification:)), name:
        Notification.Name(rawValue: NCNAME), object: nil)
    }
    @objc func receiveNotification(notification: Notification) {
        print("Notification  Received")
    }
}
```

When we use `NotificationCenter`, we have to remember to prefix the method that will be called with the `@objc` attribute. The `@objc` attribute makes our Swift API available to the Objective-C runtime. This allows us to use the `receiveNotifications()` methods with `NotificationCenter`.

We can now use these types as follows:

```
var postType = PostType()
var observerType = ObserverType()
postType.post()
```

If we run this example, we will see that the `Notification Received` message from the `ObserverType` instance is printed to the console when we execute the `post()` method on the instance of the `PostType` type. Using the notification center is a very easy and quick way to add the observer pattern to your code.

If our notifier or observer types are written in Objective-C, then we should use the notification center as shown in this example. It is also easier to notify multiple recipients with the notification center than it is with the following solutions because that functionality is built into the notification center.

This second solution demonstrates how notifications are handled in the Cocoa and Cocoa Touch framework where we register an instance of a type, which conforms to a specific protocol, to receive notifications from instances of another type. In this example, we want to be notified when a zombie turns or spots us. Let's start by defining a protocol that any type that wants to receive the notifications must conform to. This protocol will be named ZombieObserverProtocol:

```
protocol ZombieObserverProtocol {
    func turnLeft()
    func turnRight()
    func seesUs()
}
```

This protocol will require that conforming types implement the three functions defined in the protocol. These will be the methods that are called to notify us when the zombie turns or spots us.

Now let's define the observer that will receive the notifications from the Zombie type. We will name this class MyObserver and it will conform to the ZombieObserverProtocol protocol so it can receive the notifications when the zombie does something:

```
class MyObserver: ZombieObserverProtocol {
    func turnLeft() {
        print("Zombie turned left, we move right")
    }
    func turnRight() {
        print("Zombie turned right, we move left")
    }
    func seesUs() {
        print("Zombie sees us, RUN!!!!")
    }
}
```

Finally, we will implement our Zombie type. The Zombie type will send out notifications to the observer when it turns or spots someone:

```
struct Zombie {
    var observer: ZombieObserverProtocol

    func turnZombieLeft() {
        //Code to turn left
        //Notify observer
        observer.turnLeft()
    }
    func turnZombieRight() {
        //Code to turn right
```

```
            //Notify observer
            observer.turnRight()
    }
    func spotHuman() {
        //Code to lock onto a human
        //Notify observer
        observer.seesUs()
    }
}
```

In the `Zombie` type, we define one property that is of the `ZombieObserverProtocol` type. This is the instance that will receive the notifications when the zombie does something. Also in the `Zombie` type, we create three methods that are called when our zombie turns left, turns right, or spots a human. Notice that in each of the methods we notify the observer of the event that happened. Generally, these notifications would happen on new threads, but to simplify the code here we took this code out.

We would use our `Zombie` and `observer` types, as shown in the following example:

```
var observer = MyObserver()
var zombie = Zombie(observer: observer)

zombie.turnZombieLeft()
zombie.spotHuman()
```

If we ran this example, we will see that the `Zombie turned left,` `we move right,` and `Zombie sees us,` `RUN!!!!` messages from the `MyObserver` instance are printed to the console when the `turnZombieLeft()` and `spotHuman()` methods are called.

Implementing the observer pattern as shown in this example is the method used by most of the UI elements in the Cocoa and Cocoa Touch framework. If we need a single observer, this is usually the method we should use. If we need multiple observers, we could make our `observer` property an array of `MyObserver` types, but then each time we notified the observers we would need to loop through the array and notify each observer individually. It is much easier to notify multiple observers using the `NSNotificationCenter` class because the logic to call multiple observers is already implemented for us.

The third and final solution demonstrates how we would receive notifications when the value of a property is changed. This solution uses Swift's property observers feature to implement the observer pattern. Property observers, in the Swift language, observe and respond to changes to a property's value. Property observers are notified when a property's value is about to change and/or has changed.

We will begin by creating a protocol and any type that wants to receive notifications, when property changes, must conform to. This protocol will be called `PropertyObserverProtocol`:

```
protocol PropertyObserverProtocol {
    func propertyChanged(propertyName: String, newValue: Any)
}
```

This protocol defines one method named `propertyChanged()`, which will be called when the value of a property changes. This method accepts two parameters, one named `propertyName` (the name of the property) and the other named `newValue` (the new value assigned to the property).

Now let's create a type that will implement the `PropertyObserverProtocol` protocol and will be called when the value of our property changes. We will name this type `MyObserverType`:

```
class MyObserverType: PropertyObserverProtocol {
    func propertyChanged(propertyName: String, newValue: Any) {
        print("----changed----")
        print("Property Name: \(propertyName)")
        print("New Value:   \(newValue)")
    }
}
```

`MyObserverType` conforms to the `PropertyObserverProtocol` by implementing the `propertyChanged()` method. In the `propertyChanged()` method, we print out the name of the property that changed and what the new value is.

Now we will create a type that will have a property that, when the value changes, will notify an instance of the `MyObserverType` type:

```
struct PropertyObserver {
    var observer: PropertyObserverProtocol
    var property1: String {
        didSet{
            observer.propertyChanged(propertyName: "property1",
                    newValue: property1)
        }
        willSet(newValue) {
            print("Property Changing")
        }
    }
}
```

In this example, our type has a property named `observer` of the `PropertyObserverProtocol` type and another property named `property1` of the `String` type. We use the `didSet` and `willSet` observers, defined in the Swift standard library, to monitor for changes in the property. When the `didSet` observer is called, we call the `propertyChanged()` method in our observer instance to notify it that the value of the property has been changed. We would normally call the `propertyChanged()` method in our observer instance on a separate thread.

We would use code such as this:

```
var myObserver = MyObserverType()
var p = PropertyObserver(observer: myObserver, property1: "Initial String")
p.property1 = "My String"
```

If we run this code, we will see by the output that the `propertyChanged()` method of the `MyObserverType` class was called when we changed the value of the `property1` property.

We would use this solution any time that we need to be notified when the value of a property changes.

This concludes our tour of design patterns in Swift.

Summary

Design patterns are solutions to software design problems that we tend to see over and over again in real-world application design. These patterns are designed to help us create reusable and flexible code. Design patterns can also make our code easier to read and understand for other developers and also for ourselves when we look back at our code months/years later.

If we look at the examples in this chapter carefully, we will notice that one of the backbones of design patterns is the protocol. Almost all design patterns (the singleton design pattern is an exception) use protocols to help us create very flexible and reusable code.

If this was the first time that you really looked at design patterns, you probably noticed some similarities to strategies that you have used in the past in your own code. This is expected when experienced developers are first introduced to design patterns. I would also encourage you to read more about design patterns because they will definitely help you to create more flexible and reusable code.

8
Case Studies

Ever since I bought my first computer, a Commodore Vic-20, at the age of thirteen, I have been continuously learning new computer languages. I cannot count the number of computer languages that I have learned through the years. Even when I was working as a network engineer and security specialist, I learned languages such as Perl, Python, PHP, and shell scripting to automate my administrative tasks. Learning all of those languages has taught me that the best way to learn a new programming language or a programming paradigm is to come up with several small projects and figure out how to implement them in the language or programming paradigm that I was trying to learn. With that in mind, for this chapter we will take three small projects and see how we will implement them using Swift and the protocol-oriented programming paradigm. I would recommend that you read the requirements for the project and then try to implement your own solution prior to reading the solution presented in this book. This will help you to begin thinking about application design using the protocol-oriented programming paradigm. I do have one hint for you: don't forget to use design patterns in your solutions.

In this chapter, you will learn about the following topics:

- How to apply the protocol-oriented programming paradigm in real-world situations
- How to use design patterns with protocol-oriented programming to create real-world solutions

Protocol-oriented programming isn't just about using protocols, protocol extensions, or value types. It is about how we code and architect our applications and frameworks. Protocol-oriented programming with design patterns focuses on ensuring that our code base can be easily expanded and maintained.

Focusing on how we will maintain and expand our applications and frameworks in the future may sometimes seem like a waste of time with the tight deadlines we are always on; however, in the long term, the time spent on making sure our code base is easily expandable and maintainable always ends up saving us time because requirements will change and new features will be added. We need to ensure our code base is prepared for these changes.

In this chapter, we will be looking at three real-world case studies to see how we can apply the protocol-oriented paradigm with design patterns to write solutions for real-world projects. These three case studies are:

- Creating a logging service for our applications
- Creating a data access layer
- Creating a basic calculator application

In the first case study, we will look at how we will use the protocol-oriented programming paradigm to create a logging framework that can be easily maintained and expanded by our users. In the second case study, we will see how we can use the protocol-oriented programming paradigm to create a data access layer that is ready for different storage mediums. The final case study will show us how we can use the protocol-oriented programming paradigm to create a very basic calculator that we can easily expand to add additional functionality.

Let's start by looking at how we can create a logging service for our application.

Logging service

If I counted the lines of code that I have written in each language over the course of my life it would probably show that Java is the language that I have used the most. Java definitely has its good and bad points, but one of the things that I really liked about developing applications in Java is all of the different logging frameworks that are available.

These logging frameworks make it incredibly easy to turn on log messages to make debugging very easy while we are developing our application. We can then turn those debugging messages off when it is time to build the production release of our application. To do this, these logging frameworks let us define how and where we wish to log messages for predefined log levels. We can also set them to ignore certain logging levels if we do not need them. The log levels range from info (used purely for debugging) all the way up to fatal (something really bad happened).

Some of the logging frameworks that I have used with Java are Log4j, Java Logging API, and Apache Commons Logging. For this project, we will create a logging service similar to these, but with the Swift language. The first thing we need to do is to define the requirements for our logging service.

Requirements

Our logging service has several requirements, as defined in the following list:

- We will need to have multiple log levels. The log levels that our framework will support are: `Fatal`, `Error`, `Warn`, `Debug`, and `Info`.
- We will need to have multiple logging profiles. The framework will define two profiles by default: `LoggerNull` and `LoggerConsole`. The `LoggerNull` profile will do nothing with the log message (it will pretty much ignore the message and not log it anywhere) while the `LoggerConsole` will print the log message to the console.
- The user will have the ability to add their own logging profile so they can log messages to a database, a `UILabel`, or any other location they want.
- We must have the ability to configure the logging framework when the application starts and keep that configuration throughout the life cycle of the application. We do not want to force the users of our framework to reconfigure the framework every time they need to use it.
- We can assign multiple logger profiles to a single log level to give the user the ability to display or store the logs to multiple profiles.

Before reading further, based on these requirements, see what type of design you come up with. Once you have worked out your design then continue reading and compare your design to ours.

The design

We are going to separate our design into two sections. The first section will be the *logger profile* section that will contain the types that do the actual logging of the messages to a storage medium or display them. The second section will be the *logger* section that will contain the types that our applications interface with. The logger types will determine the log level of the message and then pass the message to the appropriate logger profiles to log the message. Let's start off by looking at the *logger profile* section.

We will begin the logger profile design by creating a protocol named
`LoggerProfileProtocol`. This protocol will define the interface that our logger profile
will present and any type that conforms to this protocol can be used to log messages. Our
framework, out-of-the-box, will provide two types that conform to the
`LoggerProfileProtocol` protocol. These types are the `LoggerNull` and `LoggerConsole`
types.

By starting our design with the `LoggerProfileProtocol` protocol and using the interface
exposed by the protocol to write log messages to the display/storage medium, we are
implementing polymorphism. This will allow users of our framework to add additional
logging profiles, as they need. To add these additional logging profiles, all our users need to
do is create additional types that conform to the `LoggerProfileProtocol` protocol. These
types could provide a means to log messages to any display or storage medium that
meet their requirements such as a database, file, or even a `UILabel`.

Let's look at a diagram that shows how we implement the `LoggerProfileProtocol`
protocol design. The diagram shows that we extend the `LoggerProfileProtocol` protocol
to add a method named `getCurrentDateString()`. This method will return a formatted
string that contains the current date and time. The diagram also shows the `LoggerNull` and
`LoggerConsole` types that conform to the `LoggerProfileProtocol` protocol:

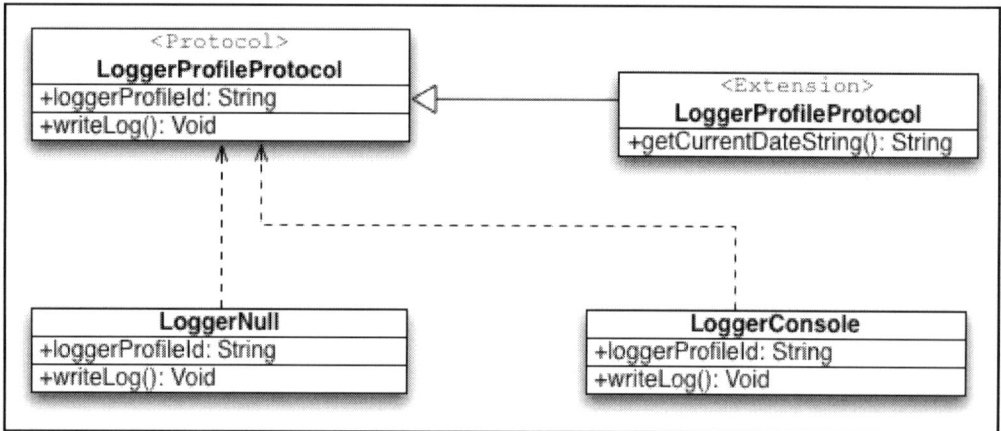

Let's look at how we implement this design. We will start off by looking at the
`LoggerProfileProtocol` protocol and the `LoggerProfileProtocol` protocol extension:

```
protocol LoggerProfileProtocol {
    var loggerProfileId: String {get}
    func writeLog(level: String, message: String)
}
```

```
extension LoggerProfileProtocol {
    func getCurrentDateString() -> String{
        let date = Date()
        let dateFormatter = DateFormatter()
        dateFormatter.dateFormat = "MM/dd/yyyy hh:mm"
        return dateFormatter.string(from: date)
    }
}
```

The `LoggerProfileProtocol` protocol defines one property and one function. The property is named `loggerProfileId`, which is of the `String` type. This property is used to uniquely identify the logging profile. We will use this property in our framework to ensure that we do not add the logger profile to any log level more than once. The method defined by our protocol is named `writeLog()` and will be called to write the log message to the display or storage medium defined by the profile.

We created a protocol extension to the `LoggerProfileProtocol` protocol to add a method named `getCurrentDateString()`. This method returns a formatted date string of the current date and time. While types that conform to the `LoggerProfileProtocol` protocol can elect not to use the `getCurrentDateString()` method provided by the protocol extension, it is recommended that they do to ensure that all logger profile types provide a date and time string with a consistent format.

Now let's look at the `LoggerNull` and `LoggerConsole` types:

```
struct LoggerNull: LoggerProfileProtocol {
    let loggerProfileId = "hoffman.jon.logger.null"
    func writeLog(level: String, message: String) {
        // Do nothing
    }
}

struct LoggerConsole: LoggerProfileProtocol {
    let loggerProfileId = "hoffman.jon.logger.console"
    func writeLog(level: String, message: String) {
        let now = getCurrentDateString()
        print("\(now): \(level) - \(message)")
    }
}
```

Both logger profiles have a unique ID defined in the `loggerProfileId` constant. We use a reverse DNS name notation as the format for this ID. Reverse DNS notation is a naming convention that is commonly used to name components, packages, and other types. A reverse DNS notation string is usually based on a registered domain name, but the names are in reverse order. For these examples, I am using my name rather than a registered domain name.

We also provide, for both types, an implementation for the `writeLog()` method that is required by the `LoggerProfileProtocol` protocol. For the `LoggerNull` type, the `writeLog()` method does not do anything because this type is designed to not write the log anywhere as if we are sending the log message to `/dev/null`. The `LoggerConsole` type retrieves a string that represents the current date and time using the `getCurrentDateString()` method provided by the `LoggerProfileProtocol` protocol extension and then writes the log message to the console.

The next part of our logger service will be the logger type, which will keep track of which logger profiles are assigned to the various log levels. Our applications will primarily use the interface provided by the logger type as the means to configure the logger service and also to log messages.

The logger types will conform to the `LoggerProtocol` protocol. While the initial design of our framework will only contain one logger type, we will still want to begin the design with the protocol to give us the ability to add additional logger types in the future. It will also give our users the ability to add additional logger types if they need to. It may not seem like that big of a deal right now, but two or three years down the road, as requirements change and new features are added, we will be glad that we used the protocol. Trust me on this one.

The first thing we need to do is to define the log levels that our framework will offer. We will use an enumeration to define these levels since there is a finite number of log levels. The following enumeration defines the log levels for our logging framework:

```
enum LogLevels: String {
case Fatal
case Error
case Warn
case Debug
case Info

static let allValues = [Fatal, Error, Warn, Debug, Info]
}
```

The `LogLevels` enumeration defines five log levels. We also provide an array that contains all five levels. This array can be used to retrieve all values in the enumeration if needed. Now let's look at our `LoggerProtocol` protocol:

```
protocol LoggerProtocol {
    static var loggers: [LogLevels:[LoggerProfileProtocol]]
        {get set}
    static func writeLog(logLevel: LogLevels, message: String)
}
```

The `LoggerProtocol` protocol defines one property named `loggers`. This property is defined to be of the `Dictionary` type whose key is a log level that is defined in the `LogLevels` enumeration and whose value is an array of types that conform to the `LoggerProfileProtocol` protocol. We also define one method in our `LoggerProtocol` protocol named `writeLog()`. This method is called within our applications to write a message to the logs and it takes two arguments. The first argument is the log level to write the log message for and the second is the log message itself.

We define both the `loggers` property and the `writeLog()` method as static so we can access them without having to create an instance of the `LoggerProtocol` type. Properties and methods that are defined with the `static` keyword are known as type properties and type methods. Another reason we create these as static is that one of the requirements for our logger framework is to be able to configure the framework once and have the ability to keep that configuration throughout the life cycle of our application. By creating these as static, there will be one (and only one) instance of them throughout the life cycle of our application, thereby fulfilling this requirement. We could have used the singleton pattern to fulfill this requirement; however, using type methods/properties would seem to work better in this situation. We will see the advantage of this when we look at how we will use our logging framework.

Now let's look at the methods that our `LoggerProtocol` protocol extension provides to types that conform to the `LoggerProtocol` protocol. Our protocol extension will provide six type (static) methods:

- `logLevelContainsProfile(logLevel: LogLevels, loggerProfile: LoggerProfileProtocol) -> Bool`: Will check the log level and return `true` if it already contains the logger profile
- `setLogLevel(logLevel: LogLevels, loggerProfile: LoggerProfileProtocol)`: Adds a logger profile to the log level
- `addLogProfileToAllLevels(defaultLoggerProfile: LoggerProfileProtocol)`: This will add the logger profile to all log levels

- removeLogProfileFromLevel(logLevel: LogLevels, loggerProfile:LoggerProfileProtocol): Removes the logger profile from the log level if it is defined for that level
- removeLogProfileFromAllLevels(loggerProfile:LoggerProfileProtoc ol): Removes the log profile from all log levels
- * hasLoggerForLevel(logLevel: LogLevels) -> Bool: Returns true if there is any logger profile configured for the log level; otherwise it returns false

Now let's look at the code for the individual methods. We will start off by looking at the logLevelContainsProfile() method:

```
static func logLevelContainsProfile(logLevel: LogLevels,
        loggerProfile: LoggerProfileProtocol) -> Bool {
    if let logProfiles = loggers[logLevel] {
        for logProfile in logProfiles where
                logProfile.loggerProfileId ==
                loggerProfile.loggerProfileId {
            return true
        }
    }
    return false
}
```

This method will return true if the log level contains the logger profile. This method is used by the setLogeLevel() and addLogProfileToAllLevels() method to ensure that we do not add a logger profile to a log level more than once. We begin this method by using optional binding to retrieve a list of logger profiles assigned to the log level. We then use the for-in statement with the where clause to loop through the list of logger profiles where the loggerProfileId property matches the loggerProfileId property of the profile we are looking for. If any item in the array matches the loggerProfileId property of the profile we are looking for, we return true; otherwise we return false.

The next method we will look at is the setLogLevel() method:

```
static func setLogLevel(logLevel: LogLevels,
    loggerProfile: LoggerProfileProtocol) {
    if let _ = loggers[logLevel] {
        if !logLevelContainsProfile(loglevel: logLevel,
    loggerProfile: loggerProfile) {
            loggers[logLevel]?.append(loggerProfile)
        }
    } else {
        var a = [LoggerProfileProtocol]()
        a.append(loggerProfile)
```

```
            loggers[logLevel] = a
    }
}
```

The setLogLevel() method will use the logLevelContainsProfile() method to verify
that the logger profile is not already assigned to the specified log level; if it isn't then it will
add the logger profile to that level. We begin this method by using optional binding to
retrieve the list of logger profiles assigned to the log level. We do this simply to verify that
there is a valid array assigned to the log level. We then use the
logLevelContainsProfile() method to verify that the logger profile is not already
assigned to the level and, if not, we add it.

If the optional binding fails at the start of the method then we create a new array, add the
logger profile to it, and assign the array to the log level within the loggers dictionary.

Now let's look at the addLogProfileToAllLevels() method:

```
static func addLogProfileToAllLevels(
    defaultLoggerProfile: LoggerProfileProtocol) {
    for level in LogLevels.allValues {
        setLogLevel(logLevel: level, loggerProfile: defaultLoggerProfile)
    }
}
```

The addLogProfileToAllLevels() method is used to add a logger profile to all log
levels. This can be used to initialize the logger framework by adding a single profile to all
levels. In this method, we loop through each of the log levels and then call the
setLogLevel() method to try to add the logger profile to each of the individual log levels.

The next method we will look at is the removeLogProfileFromLevel() method:

```
static func removeLogProfileFromLevel(logLevel: LogLevels,
loggerProfile:LoggerProfileProtocol) {
    if var logProfiles = loggers[logLevel] {
        if let index = logProfiles.index(where:
{$0.loggerProfileId == loggerProfile.loggerProfileId}) {
            logProfiles.remove(at: index)
        }
        loggers[logLevel] = logProfiles
    }
}
```

The `removeLogProfileFromLevel()` method will remove the logger profile from the specified log level. This method starts off by using optional binding to retrieve the list of logger profiles for the log level. We then use the `indexOf()` method to locate the index of the logger profile that matches the logger profile that we want to remove (it will return `nil` if it cannot find a match). If we find the profile we then remove it.

The next method is the `removeLogProfileFromAllLevels()` method:

```
static func
removeLogProfileFromAllLevels(loggerProfile:LoggerProfileProtocol) {
    for level in LogLevels.allValues {
        removeLogProfileFromLevel(logLevel: level,
loggerProfile: loggerProfile)
    }
}
```

The `removeLogProfileFromAllLevels()` method will attempt to remove a logger profile from all log levels. This method will loop through all of the log levels that we have defined and call the `removeLogProfileFromLevel()` method in an attempt to remove the logger profile from the level.

The final method in our `LoggerProtocol` protocol extension is the `hasLoggerForLevel()` method:

```
static func hasLoggerForLevel(logLevel: LogLevels) -> Bool {
    guard let _ = loggers[logLevel] else {
        return false
    }
    return true
}
```

The `hasLoggerForLevel()` method returns `true` if the log level contains any logger profiles; otherwise, it returns `false`. This method uses optional binding with a guard statement to retrieve the list of logger profiles assigned to the log level. If the optional binding statement fails then a `false` value is returned; otherwise, a `true` value is returned.

Now let's look at our `Logger` type, which will conform to the `LoggerProtocol` protocol:

```
struct Logger: LoggerProtocol {
    static var loggers = [LogLevels:[LoggerProfileProtocol]]()
    static func writeLog(logLevel: LogLevels, message: String) {
        guard hasLoggerForLevel(logLevel: logLevel) else {
            print("No logger")
            return
        }
        if let logProfiles = loggers[logLevel] {
```

```
        for logProfile in logProfiles {
            logProfile.writeLog(level: logLevel.rawValue, message:
                    message)
        }
    }
}
}
```

The `Logger` type is the type that we use in our application for configuration of our log levels and also for logging our messages. The `Logger` type conforms to the `LoggerProtocol` protocol by implementing the requirements defined by the protocol.

The `Logger` type has one property named `loggers` that is a dictionary whose key is a log level defined in the `LogLevels` enumeration and whose value is an array of types that conform to the `LoggerProfileProtocol` protocol. The `writeLog()` method is used within our applications to write a message to the log and it takes two arguments. The first argument is the log level to write the log message for and the second is the log message itself.

The `writeLog()` method checks to see if we have any log profiles assigned to the log level and if so we loop through the list of profiles and call the `writeLog()` method on each profile, passing it the message we wish to log.

We could now use our logger framework as follows:

```
Logger.addLogProfileToAllLevels(LoggerConsole())
Logger.writeLog(LogLevels.Debug, message: "Debug Message 1")")

Logger.setLogLevel(logLevel: LogLevels.Error,
        loggerProfile: LoggerDataBase())
Logger.setLogLevel(logLevel: LogLevels.Fatal,
        loggerProfile: LoggerDataBase())
Logger.writeLog(LogLevels.Error, message: "Error Message 1")")
```

In this sample code, we begin by adding the `LoggerConsole` logger profile to all of our log levels. This will cause all log messages, no matter what the log level is, to be logged to the console. We then write a log message (`Debug Message 1`) with the log level set to `Debug`. This log message will be printed to the console.

In the next couple of lines, we will add the LoggerDatabase logger profile (this will be a user created profile) to both the Error and Fatal log levels. The LoggerDatabase logger profile will be a profile that logs messages to a database such as SQLite and will need to conform to the LoggerProfileProtocol protocol. We then write the log message ErrorMessage 1 with the log level set to Error. This will write the log message to both the console and database since both logger profiles are assigned to the Error log level.

In this example, we can see that we do not need to create an instance of the Logger type to configure it or to log messages. The reason for this is that we made the properties and methods static (type methods and type properties). When we are creating frameworks that should have a very small footprint, for instance our logger framework, using type methods and properties to avoid instantiation of our types can make our frameworks significantly easier to use.

Conclusion

The basis of both the logger profiles and the logger itself are protocols. We also use protocol extensions to add functionality to types that will conform to our protocol; therefore, it is very easy to add additional profiles and loggers by creating new types that conform to these protocols. These new types also automatically receive the functionality defined in our protocol extensions. Designing our framework in this manner allows us to very easily add functionality and new features as we receive new requirements. It also allows users of our framework to expand it to suit their needs.

When designing frameworks or applications, one thing that all good architects keep in the back of their mind is not only implementing the current requirements, but also how they can expand the framework or application to meet future needs. This is the idea behind using protocols and using the interface provided by the protocol rather than concrete types. If we use the interface provided by the protocol, we have the ability to use any type that conforms to the protocol, giving us the ability to very easily expand the framework or application to meet future needs.

Now let's look at how we can create a data access layer that can be easily expanded to use different data storage mediums.

Data access layer

Most serious applications need to persist some amount of data. This data could be transactional data, user preferences, or the current state of the application. There are many ways that we can persist data in our applications and figuring out the appropriate way to persist it can be one of the most critical decisions that an architect needs to make.

As an architect, we should separate the actual data storage from our business logic. This will allow us, in the future, to change how our data is persisted without having to change our business logic. This is called a **data access layer**.

It is important when designing an application, to design a good data access layer. Having a good data access layer will make our code much easier to maintain as requirements change. As an example of this, let's say that we choose to persist our data in an XML formatted file and then we embed the code to access this file in multiple parts of our code. In the future, if we decided to switch to a database backend, rather than the XML file, we would have to refactor multiple parts of our code base to access this new database. If we separate our data access layer from our main business logic, then if our backend data store changes, we will only need to change the code in our data access layer.

Requirements

Our data access layer will have several requirements:

- All access to the backend data storage should go through the data helper types. These data helper types will handle all of the **Create, Read, Update, Delete (CRUD)** functionality to the backend storage.
- Code external to this data access layer should not know or care how the data is persisted.
- For our example, we will need to create two types, one named `player` that will contain information about a baseball player and one named `team` that will contain information about a baseball team. Each baseball player will contain the Team ID and information about the team that they play for.
- For our example, we will store the data in an array; however, we will need the ability to change the storage mechanism without having to touch our business logic code.

Before reading further, based on these requirements, see what type of design you come up with. Once you have worked out your design, continue reading and compare your design to the one we present.

The design

Our data access layer will consist of three layers. The bottom-most layer, known as the **Data Helper Layer**, will consist of classes that will be used to persist our data. For this example, the data will be stored in an array, but the classes should be easily updatable to persist the data any way we need to in the future.

The next layer is the **Data Model Layer**, which will contain tuples that model pretty closely to how we wish to store our data. These tuples will be used as temporary storage to read and write data to/from the data store. Some people prefer using structures at the model layer, but I find that tuples work just as well because we do not want any business logic embedded within this layer. Keep in mind that these layers are purely for data access because we want to maintain good separation between our data access code and our application logic.

The next layer is the **Bridge Layer**, which converts the data from the business logic layer into the data access layer. The bridge layer is the layer that separates our business logic from the data access logic. This layer will need to contain types that our business logic will use to access the data from our data access layer. It will also contain bridge types that will convert the data types used in the business access layer to the data types used in the data access layer.

In our example, we will have two types. These are the `Teams` and the `Players` tables. From the preceding description, we can probably guess that this means we will need two data helper classes (`TeamDataHelper` and `PlayerDataHelper`) and two tuples (`Team` and `Player`). The data access layer design will look like this:

Bridge Layer	PlayerBridge / Player	TeamBridge / Team
Data Model Layer	PlayerData	TeamData
Data Helper Layer	PlayerDataHelper	TeamDataHelper

Let's start off by looking at the data model layer since it will be the communication layer between the bridge layer and the data helper layer.

Data model layer

In our data model layer, we will need to define two types that will model the data in our data store. These types will be used to transfer the data from our data access layer to the rest of our code. Since these types should be used exclusively to transfer the data, using value types is definitely preferred. The reason why we should avoid using these types in our business logic layer is that we do not want to tightly couple our business logic with the data structures in our data access layer. If we do not tightly couple our business logic with our data access layer, we have the ability to change either one independently of the other. With this in mind, we will use tuples to model our data, as shown in the following code:

```
typealias TeamData = (
    teamId: Int64?,
    city: String?,
    nickName: String?,
    abbreviation: String?
)

typealias PlayerData = (
    playerId: Int64?,
    firstName: String?,
    lastName: String?,
    number: Int?,
    teamId: Int64?,
    position: Positions?
)
```

To emphasize this again, it is important as an architect to avoid using these types in our business logic layer. We will have a bridge that will convert the data from these types into data structures used by the business logic layer. We will implement these bridges later in this section.

In our `Player` tuple, we have an element named `position` of the `Positions` type. The `Positions` type is an enumeration that contains all of the valid positions that a player can play. The following code shows how we define the `Positions` type:

```
enum Positions: String {
    case Pitcher = "Pitcher"
    case Catcher = "Catcher"
    case FirstBase = "First Base"
    case SecondBase = "Second Base"
    case ThirdBase = "Third Base"
    case Shortstop = "Shortstop"
    case LeftField = "Left Field"
    case CenterField = "Center Field"
    case RightField = "Right field"
```

```
        case DesignatedHitter = "Designated Hitter"
    }
```

Now let's look at our data helper layer that will be used to persist our data.

Data helper layer

In a design such as this, we want to make sure we have good error checking that will let us know what went wrong if something bad happens. With this in mind, we will start our data helper layer by defining the errors that can be thrown. We will be using Swift's error handling framework, therefore our errors are defined in an enumeration as follows:

```
enum DataAccessError: ErrorType {
    case Datastore_Connection_Error
    case Insert_Error
    case Delete_Error
    case Search_Error
    case Nil_In_Data
}
```

We will see how these errors are thrown as we go through the code. Depending on the type of persistence we use, the error types may change to give more details about the actual errors that occurred.

The data helper layer will be used to persist our data. This is the layer that will change as our storage mechanism changes. In this example, we will be storing the data in an array; however, the types in this layer should have the ability to change as different storage mechanism are needed in the future. This layer will contain one type for each data type in our data model layer. These types will be used to read and write our data.

We will begin by creating a data helper protocol that will define the minimum set of methods that each data helper class needs to implement. We define this protocol so that months/years from now when we are making changes to our data access layer, we will know what minimum set of methods are expected within our data helper classes. The DataHelperProtocol protocol looks as follows:

```
protocol DataHelperProtocol {
    typealias T
    static func insert(_ item: T) throws -> Int64
    static func delete(_ item: T) throws -> Void
    static func findAll() throws -> [T]?
}
```

Within this protocol, we define three methods. These are:

- `insert`: Inserts a row into the table
- `delete`: Deletes a row from the table
- `findAll`: Returns all rows in the table

Notice that we only define one method to query our data stores. We do this because the methods to query each individual data type may vary depending on our data; therefore, the method(s) needed to query these types could be different. We need to evaluate the query method(s) needed for each data type on an individual basis.

Now let's build the `TeamDataHelper` class that will conform to the `DataHelperProtocol` protocol. This class will be used to persist our data:

```
class TeamDataHelper: DataHelperProtocol {
// Code goes here
}
```

We will start the class off by defining the array to store our data in and the `typealias`, as shown here:

```
typealias T = TeamData
static var teamData: [T] = []
```

We define the `teamData` array as static so there will be one and only one instance of this array in our code. The `typealias` `T` is set to the `TeamData` type. The `typealias` of `T` is used within our protocol to define the type to use within the concrete type. Now let's look at how we implement each of the three methods defined in the `DataHelperProtocol` protocol plus one extra method that will search the data by its unique identifier. We will not discuss the implementation details here because we are more concerned with the design rather than how we store/search information in an array.

The first method that we will implement is the `insert()` method, which will insert an item into our array. This method will return an `Int64` value representing the unique ID of the item if everything was stored properly. This method will also throw an error if there is an issue with the data. If we were using another storage mechanism besides an array, we may throw additional errors if we had an issue storing the data:

```
static func insert(_ item: T) throws -> Int64 {
guard item.teamId != nil && item.city != nil &&
item.nickName != nil && item.abbreviation != nil
else {
      throw DataAccessError.nil_In_Data
   }
```

```
        teamData.append(item)
        return item.teamId!
    }
```

Now let's create the `delete()` function to remove an item from the array. This method will throw an error if the item does not exist in the database or if the `teamId` is `nil`:

```
static func delete (_ item: T) throws -> Void {
    guard let id = item.teamId else {
        throw DataAccessError.nil_In_Data
    }
    let teamArray = teamData
for (index, team) in teamArray.enumerated() where team.teamId ==  id {
        teamData.remove(at: index)
        return
    }
    throw DataAccessError.delete_Error
}
```

Now we will implement the `findAll()` method, which will return all of the teams in the array. This method can throw an error, but that is more for future needs:

```
static func findAll() throws -> [T]? {
    return teamData
}
```

Finally, we will implement the `find()` method to search and return a single item from the team array. We may need additional find methods depending on our needs, but this method will return the team with the particular `teamId`. This method is also marked that it will throw an error, but it is also for future needs. If the `teamId` is not found in the array it will return a `nil` value:

```
static func find(_ id: Int64) throws -> T? {
    for team in teamData where team.teamId == id {
        return team
    }
    return nil
}
```

The `PlayerDataHelper` class is implemented just like the `TeamDataHelper` class. To see the code for the `PlayerDataHelper` class, please download the code from the Packt Publishing website.

If we were so inclined, we could use the data (`PlayerData` and `TeamData`) and data helper (`PlayerDataHelper` and `TeamDataHelper`) types directly, as shown in the following example; however, as we mentioned earlier, that would be very unwise:

```
let bosId = try? TeamDataHelper.insert(
TeamData(
teamId: 0,
city: "Boston",
nickName: "Red Sox",
abbreviation: "BOS"))
print(bosId)

let ortizId = try? PlayerDataHelper.insert(
PlayerData(
playerId: 0,
firstName: "David",
lastName: "Ortiz",
number: 34,
teamId: bosId,
position: Positions.DesignatedHitter))
print(ortizId)
```

The reason we would not want to access the data helper types directly in our application code is that we would be tightly coupling the data access layer to our application layer. If we received new requirements that required us to modify the data access layer then we would have to refactor large parts of our code. This would make it hard to maintain or expand our data access layer to meet future requirements.

If we look through the design patterns that we discussed earlier in this book, we will see that the bridge pattern could help us out here. Let's see how we will use the bridge pattern to maintain a good separation layer between our data access layer and our application code.

We need to start off by defining how we wish to model our data within our application. We can model it exactly like the data model for our database or we can design it significantly differently.

 I usually find that if I properly normalize my data in the database, there are usually significant differences between how I store my data and how I use it within my application. By separating our data access layer from our application code, we are also able to model our data differently between these two layers.

Let's now look at how we would design our bridge layer.

Bridge layer

In our example, the data in the data access layer and the application layer will have one small difference, but other than that it is pretty much the same. The difference will be when we enter a team ID for a player; the information about that team will be retrieved and will be a part of the player's data structure. Let's see how we would do this by looking at how we would represent the team and player in our code:

```
struct Team {
    var teamId: Int64?
    var city: String?
    var nickName:String?
    var abbreviation:String?
    init(teamId: Int64?, city: String?, nickName: String?,
    abbreviation: String?) {
        self.teamId = teamId
        self.city = city
        self.nickName = nickName
        self.abbreviation = abbreviation
    }
}
```

In our example here, we are using value types for our data structures in our applications in line with Apple's recommendations. When we use value types for data structures such as this, we need to remember that changes to these types are only persisted in the scope that the changes are made in. If we need to persist the changes outside the scope the changes were made in, we must use `inout` parameters, as we will see later in this section. Ultimately, the choice between using a value or reference types is yours; the key is to be consistent and document the type used so it is easy for other developers to know what type was used.

In this example, the `Team` structure is designed to mirror the `TeamData` tuple that represents the teams in our database. We do not actually need to implement the initializer in this example because with structures, we already receive this initializer; however, we implement it here for consistency purposes because we need to implement an initializer for our `Player` structure. Now let's look at the `Player` structure:

```
struct Player {
    var playerId: Int64?
    var firstName: String?
    var lastName: String?
    var number: Int?
    var teamId: Int64? {
        didSet {
            if let t = try? TeamBridge.retrieve(teamId!) {
```

```
                    team = t
                }
            }
        }
    var position: Positions?
    var team: Team?
init(playerId: Int64?, firstName: String?, lastName: String?, number:
Int?, teamId: Int64?, position: Positions?) {
        self.playerId = playerId
        self.firstName = firstName
        self.lastName = lastName
        self.number = number
        self.teamId = teamId
        self.position = position
        if let id = self.teamId {
            if let t = try? TeamBridge.retrieve(id) {
                team = t
            }
        }
    }
}
```

The `Player` structure is also similar to the `PlayerData` tuple, except we add an additional optional property of the `Team` type. This property will hold the information about the team that the player is on. We use a property observer to load the information about the team from the database whenever the `teamId` property is set. We also load the team information in the initializer. Remember that the property observers are not called during initialization of a type; therefore, the `didSet` observer is not called when we set the `teamId` during initialization.

Now let's look at the bridge types that will be used as a bridge between our data access layer and our application code. We will start off with our `TeamBridge` structure:

```
struct TeamBridge {
    static func save(_ team:inout Team) throws {
        let teamData = toTeamData(team)
        let id = try TeamDataHelper.insert(teamData)
        team.teamId = id
    }
    static func delete(_ team:Team) throws {
        let teamData = toTeamData(team)
        try TeamDataHelper.delete(teamData)
    }
    static func retrieve(_ id: Int64) throws -> Team? {
        if let t = try TeamDataHelper.find(id) {
            return toTeam(t)
        }
```

```
            return nil
        }
    static func toTeamData(_ team: Team) -> TeamData {
        return TeamData(teamId: team.teamId , city: team.city,
            nickName: team.nickName, abbreviation:
            team.abbreviation)
    }
    static func toTeam(_ teamData: TeamData) -> Team {
        return Team(teamId: teamData.teamId, city: teamData.city,
            nickName: teamData.nickName, abbreviation:
            teamData.abbreviation)
    }
}
```

The `TeamBridge` structure has five methods. The first three methods use the functionality from the `TeamDataHelper` structure to insert, delete, and retrieve data from our data access layer. Notice in the `save()` method that we use an `inout` parameter because we are making changes to the `team` parameter that we want to persist outside of the scope for this method. The last two methods will convert the data between the `TeamData` tuple (data access layer) and the `Team` class (application layer). Now if (when) our requirements change, we can change either the data access layer or the application layer independently of the other. The bridge structure may need to change as either the data access layer or the application layer changes, but it is a lot easier to make this change in one part of our code rather than refactoring our entire code base.

Now let's see the `PlayerBridge` structure:

```
struct PlayerBridge {
    static func save(_ player:inout Player) throws {
        let playerData = toPlayerData(player)
        let id = try PlayerDataHelper.insert(playerData)
        player.playerId = id
    }
    static func delete(_ player:Player) throws {
        let playerData = toPlayerData(player)
        try PlayerDataHelper.delete(playerData)
    }
    static func retrieve(_ id: Int64) throws -> Player? {
        if let p = try PlayerDataHelper.find(id) {
            return toPlayer(p)
        }
        return nil
    }
    static func toPlayerData(_ player: Player) -> PlayerData {
        return PlayerData(playerId: player.playerId, firstName:
player.firstName, lastName: player.lastName,
```

```
number: player.number, teamId: player.teamId,
position: player.position)
    }
    static func toPlayer(_ playerData: PlayerData) -> Player {
        return Player(playerId: playerData.playerId, firstName:
playerData.firstName, lastName: playerData.lastName, number:
playerData.number, teamId: playerData.teamId, position:
playerData.position)
    }
}
```

As we can see, the `PlayerBridge` structure is very similar to the `TeamBridge` structure, except that we are converting between the `PlayerData` tuple (data access layer) and the `Player` class (application layer). Once again this allows us to change either the data access layer or the application layer independently of the other.

Using the data access layer

We will use the data access layer by using the `Team` and `Player` types as entities and the `TeamBridge` and `PlayerBridge` types for our create/retrieve/delete functionality. We will create new entities, as shown in the following code:

```
var bos = Team(
teamId: 0,
city: "Boston",
nickName: "Red Sox",
abbreviation: "BOS")

try? TeamBridge.save(&bos)

var ortiz = Player(
playerId: 0,
firstName: "David",
lastName: "Ortiz",
number: 34,
teamId: bos.teamId,
position: Positions.DesignatedHitter)

try? PlayerBridge.save(&ortiz)
```

In this code, we created one team, the Boston Red Sox and one player, David Ortiz. We also put David Ortiz on the Boston Red Sox team, but we assigned the `teamId` to the `teamId`, giving it to the Red Sox team. We can now retrieve this information, as shown in the following code:

```
if let team = try? TeamBridge.retrieve(0) {
    print("--- \(team?.city)")
}

if let player = try? PlayerBridge.retrieve(0) {
print("---- \(player?.firstName) \(player?.lastName) plays for
    (player?.team?.city)")
}
```

This code will print out the following results:

```
--- Optional("Boston")")
---- Optional("David")") Optional("Ortiz")") plays for Optional("Boston")")
```

As we can see, by using the `TeamBridge` and `TeamPlayer` types, we do not need to be concerned about how the data is being stored in the backend. It can use an SQLite database, an array, or even a file to store the information. We are also able to change the backend storage to use any mechanism that we want without having to change any of the frontend code. This will allow us to change our backend storage to meet any new requirements that we may have in the future with having to refactor all of our frontend code.

Conclusion

Creating separate layers, as we showed in this example, may take additional time when we initially build our application, but it will save us time over the long term because requirements will change and new features will be added; therefore, our code needs to be easy to change to meet these needs. Creating separate layers, and using the bridge pattern to connect these layers, gives us the ability to change either layer easily and independently of the other.

For our third and final case study, we will be creating a very modest calculator application.

Calculator application

In this case study, we will create a very simple calculator application. This application will give the user the ability to add, subtract, multiply, and divide whole or decimal numbers.

We will not go through how to set up the application or the UI design in this section. We will leave that up to you. This will let you design the UI as you want to and also allow you to build the application as an iOS or an OS X application. You could even build it as a Linux-based application since Swift is now open source.

You can download the iOS calculator application with the code bundle for this book. My design looks similar to the following screenshot:

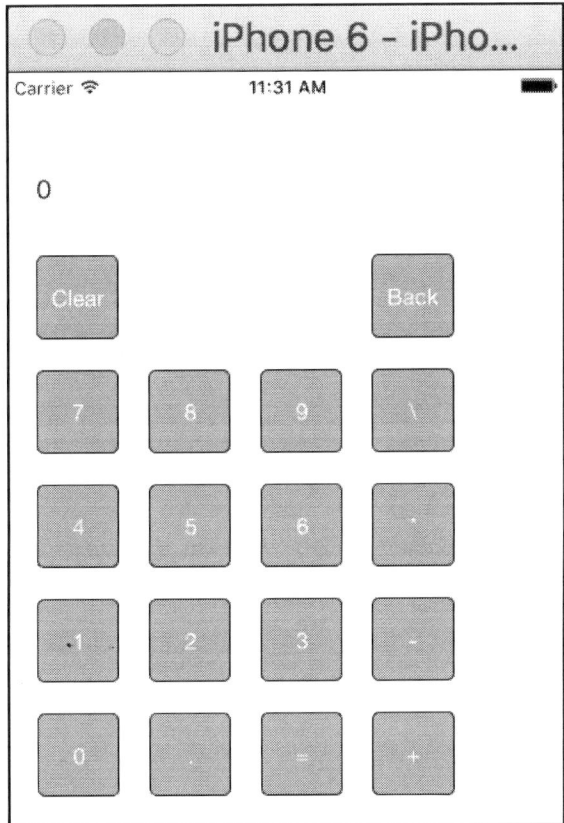

Now let's look at the requirements.

Requirements

Here are the requirements for our application:

- The calculator needs the ability to add, subtract, multiply, and divide
- We need the ability to clear the current calculation
- We need the ability to clear the last number pressed
- We need to be able to display the value of the current calculation
- We need buttons for the numbers 0 through 9
- We need a button for a decimal point

Before reading further, based on these requirements, see what type of design you come up with. Once you have worked out your design, continue reading and compare your design with the one we present.

The design

The underlying philosophy behind our design is going to be making it easy to add new features in the future. We may be starting off with a basic calculator, but eventually we will probably want to add additional features such as sine, cosine, tangent, or other scientific functions. Just like the `SQLite.swift` case study, there is a design pattern that can help us. The pattern we will use for this calculator example is the command pattern.

In order to understand how to design our commands, we need to understand how our calculator should work. The following steps should achieve this:

1. The calculator current value is 0.
2. The user presses the [2] button: The number 2 should be displayed.
3. The user presses the [5] button: The display should now read 25.
4. The user presses the [+] button: Since 25 (what is being displayed) is the first number in the calculation, we set the current value for the calculation to 25 and clear the display.
5. The user presses the [5] button: The display should now read 5.
6. The user presses the [=] button: The calculator will add the number that is displayed to its current value for the calculation since the last command key that was pressed was the addition key. The calculator will set this new value as its current value and then display it. The display now reads 30.

What these steps show us is that each time the user presses a number button, we update the display. Whenever the user presses a command button (addition, subtraction, multiplication, division, or equals) we need to perform the function from the last command key that was pressed on the calculator's current value with the number that is currently being displayed.

So let's look at how we will write our command structures. We will need to start by creating a protocol that all command types must conform to. The following code shows what our command protocol looks like:

```
protocol CommandProtocol {
    func execute(firstValue: Double, secondValue:Double) -> Double
}
```

This protocol defines a method named `execute`. This method will take two values of the `Double` type, perform some function on those two numbers, and then return a new value of the `Double` type. This method is designed to encapsulate the logic needed to perform the mathematical function represented by the command type and return the results.

Now let's look at our addition, subtraction, multiplication, and division types that will conform to the command protocol that we just defined:

```
struct AddCommand: CommandProtocol {
    func execute(firstValue: Double, secondValue: Double) -> Double {
        return firstValue + secondValue
    }
}

struct SubCommand: CommandProtocol {
    func execute(firstValue: Double, secondValue: Double) -> Double {
        return firstValue - secondValue
    }
}

struct MultiplyCommand: CommandProtocol {
    func execute(firstValue: Double, secondValue: Double) -> Double {
        return firstValue * secondValue
    }
}

struct DivideCommand: CommandProtocol {
    func execute(firstValue: Double, secondValue: Double) -> Double {
        return firstValue / secondValue
    }
}
```

Each of these command types conform to the CommandProtocol protocol by implementing the execute() method. The execute() method performs the appropriate function on the two values that are passed in and then returns the results.

Now let's create our Calculator type, which will use the command types to perform our calculations:

```
struct Calculator {
    var currentValue: Double = 0.0
    var lastCommand: CommandProtocol?
    mutating func clear() {
        currentValue = 0.0
    }
    mutating func commandEntered(newNumber: Double,
            nextCommand: CommandProtocol?) {
        if let lastCommand = self.lastCommand {
            self.currentValue = lastCommand.execute(firstValue:
                        currentValue, secondValue: newNumber)
        } else {
            self.currentValue = newNumber
        }
        lastCommand = nextCommand
    }
}
```

Our Calculator type has two properties. The first property is of the Double type and it is named currentValue. This property will keep track of the current value of our calculation. The second property is an optional of the CommandProtocol type and it is named lastCommand. This property will store the last command submitted to the calculator.

We have two methods in our Calculator structure. The first method, named clear(), simply sets the currentValue property to 0. The second method, named commandEntered(), accepts two arguments. The first argument of the Double type is named newNumber and the second argument of the CommandProtocol type is nextCommand.

The commandEntered method starts off by checking to see if the lastCommand property contains an instance of a type that conforms to the CommandProtocol. If it does contain an instance, we will call the execute() method of the instance. The execute() method will perform some functionality and then returns a new value. This new value will then be set as the current value for the calculator. The calculator does not know, or care, exactly what function the execute() method will perform; all it knows is that it needs to call that method. This is how the command pattern is designed to work.

Now let's see how we will use the `Calculator` class by looking at how we use it in the iOS example that comes with the downloaded code for this book. In this example, we use instances of the `UIbutton` class for each of the buttons on our calculator. In the `UIButton` class, we have a property named `tag` that we can use to assign a unique number to each of our buttons that identifies the button that was tapped. In our example, the following tags are assigned to each button:

Tag	Button
0	Equals button
1	Addition Button
2	Subtraction Button
3	Multiplication Button
4	Division Button
5	Clear Button

The method that handles the touch events for the command buttons looks as follows:

```
@IBAction func commandButtonTapped(sender: UIButton) {
    if let text = display.text, num = Double(text) {
        var clearDisplay = true
        switch sender.tag {
        case 0:
            calculator.commandEntered(newNumber: num, nextCommand: nil)
            display.text = "\(calculator.currentValue)"
            clearDisplay = false
        case 1:
            calculator.commandEntered(newNumber: num, nextCommand:
                AddCommand())
        case 2:
            calculator.commandEntered(newNumber: num, nextCommand:
                SubCommand())
        case 3:
            calculator.commandEntered(newNumnber: num, nextCommand:
                MultiplyCommand())
        case 4:
            calculator.commandEntered(newNumber: num, nextCommand:
                DivideCommand())
        case 5:
            calculator.clear()
        default:
            break
        }
        if clearDisplay {
```

```
            display.text = "0"
        }
      }
   }
```

Within the `CommandButtonTapped()` method, we use a switch statement to pick the button that was tapped. We then call the `commandEntered()` method of the `Calculator` instance and pass it the current number that is being displayed (entered by the user) and an instance of the appropriate command type.

Conclusion

When we need to add additional functionality to our calculator, all we need to do is to create additional types that conform to the `CommandProtocol` protocol that encapsulates the logic for this new functionality. We are then able to pass instances of these new types to our calculator. The ability to easily add new functionality to our applications is what makes the command pattern so powerful.

Summary

In this chapter, we looked at three case studies to see how we can use Swift with the protocol-oriented programming paradigm and how to use design patterns to create easy-to-maintain and very flexible applications. If you worked through the designs yourself and your design was different from the ones we presented here, that is ok. There are many correct answers for each of the problems. The key is to make sure your applications are designed to be easily maintained and very flexible.

As an architect, your focus should not only be on meeting the requirements of your framework or application, but also on making your code base easy to maintain and expand to meet future requirements. Using a programming paradigm such as protocol-oriented programming and emphasizing the use of design patterns in our application's design can help us meet these requirements.

Index

Printed in Great Britain
by Amazon